29.95

Theater Festivals

Best Worldwide Venues for New Works

Lisa Mulcahy

ALLWORTH PRESS
NEW YORK

08 07 06 05 04   5 4 3 2 1

Published by Allworth Press
An imprint of Allworth Communications, Inc.
10 East 23rd Street, New York, NY 10010

Cover design by Derek Bacchus

Interior design by

Page composition/typography by
Cover Photo Credit: LUMA®, See You in the Dark (*www.lumatheatre.com*)

ISBN: 1-58115-402-X

Library of Congress Cataloging-in-Publication Data

Mulcahy, Lisa.
    Theater festivals: best worldwide venues for new works/Lisa Mulcahy.
    p. cm.
    Includes index.
    ISBN 1-58115-402-X (pbk.)
1. Drama festivals.   2. Performing arts festivals.   I. Title.

PN3156.M86 2005
792'.079—dc22

                                                                    2004029551

Printed in Canada

— For my father, William Mulcahy —

Acknowledgments

I'd like to express my heartfelt thanks to the following people who helped me immeasurably during the genesis of this book:

As always, I salute my guiding forces at Allworth Press, Tad Crawford and Nicole Potter-Talling, for their belief in my work, incredible input, and invaluable support. I'd also like to commend the crackerjack Allworth staff as a whole, who all are a pleasure to work with, and give a special mention to Michael Madole, whose positive professionalism is simply terrific, and Jessica Rozler, for all of her terrific contributions.

My deepest appreciation goes out to the festival artists and industry leaders who graciously and generously share their insights and expertise within these pages: Melody Brooks, Shannan Calcutt, Leah Cooper, Zan Sawyer Dailey, TJ Dawe, Bob Dolan, Charles Fee, David Fuller, Kristen Gandrow, Christopher Lee Gibson, Patrick Goddard, Steven Gove, Matt Grabowski, Paul Gudgin, Stella Hall, Ed Herendeen, Kim Peter Kovac, Fergus Linehan, Jenny Magnus, Joseph Melillo, Thomas Morrissey, Janet Munsil, Trey Nichols, Nigel Redden, Charlie Ross, Mark Scharf, Kirsten Schrader, Kate Snodgrass, Nick Stucchio, Jason R. Teeter, Jon Tuttle, Daniella Topol, Susan Woolverton, and Sue Zizza.

My gratitude also goes out to the following festival personnel who aided me greatly in working out the logistics of numerous interviews: Graeme Farrow, Marie Jacinto Lawson, Shoshana Polanco, Martin Reynolds, Kyle Shepherd, Wanda Snyder, Marie Storey, and David Wanger. Extra-special thanks for extra-special assistance goes to Elena Holy, Owen O'Leary, Beth Marshall, and again, Martin Reynolds; plus Angela Pfenninger for providing me with supplementary materials.

A very special mention to the lovely Vivion Stinson, Shannel Stinson-Davis, Sally Dickinson, Noelle Dickinson, Helen Kenny, and Virginia Farillas. Your grace, generosity, and kindness is an inspiration to me and everyone lucky enough to know you.

I would like to give special thanks as well to Bob Dolan and Lynn Marie Macy.

I would like to give very, very special thanks to Donna L. Fougere, Publishing Specialist, without whose help this project would not be possible.

For her technical wizardry, I thank Johanne Cimon of The Most Office in Fitchburg, Massachusetts; her work is, as always, fantastic. Special kudos also go out to my aunt, Sr. Joan Mulcahy, for communications assistance, and to my cousin, Sandy Falk, for providing the book's mascot.

I thank my entire family, the extended Mulcahy and Kelly clans, for their never-ending love and support. To my posse of friends, thanks for always being there. I send out gratitude and best wishes to the Brandeis University community, my dear friends and colleagues on the New York City theater scene, and to my past mentors Ted Kazanoff and Edward Albee.

Most of all, I thank my beloved mom, Joan Mulcahy, who means the world to me.

—LISA MULCAHY

Contents

INTRODUCTION

The Festival World—
Originality Meets
Opportunity

The need to be seen and heard: That's the motivation that drives virtually every theater artist.

You'd think that when you're dealing with an entity as important as art, the world would be hanging on every quality playmaker's word, but sadly, we know this just isn't the case. You could blame this on the fact that our culture seems to want nothing more visionary or intelligent out of its entertainment than watching Playboy Playmates eat giant bugs on *Fear Factor*, but that's not the whole problem. Really, the issue is lack of opportunity: Where is the work of a smart, risk-taking writer, performer, or director really welcome these days?

As commercial theater's sensibility becomes more conservative—there are more revivals and Disney-fied musicals in New York these days than you can shake a stick at—there's less and less room for the kind of trailblazing stuff that pushes the art form to a new level. That's not to say a lot of those revivals and Disney-fied productions aren't worthwhile—they fill seats, introduce new generations to the theater, and actually can be pretty good. Still, we always need a safe haven for daring material. And that's getting harder and harder to find, as more and more regional companies also turn a blind eye to the original, for the sake of placating their subscriber bases.

All's far from lost, however: The world of new works festivals offers an invaluable oasis for both artists *and* receptive audiences. Working at a theater festival, in the best-case scenario, can allow you to maintain total control over your material (even allowing you the option of developing or reworking it on its feet as part of the performance process). It can provide you with a huge swell of patrons who'll have definite reactions, either positive or negative, to your work, and won't be the least bit shy about letting you know what they think. It can allow you the rare luxury of unlimited networking (with producers or scouts who might want to option your show, or talented fellow artists with whom you could fruitfully collaborate). It can give you the chance to actually make some cash doing what you love most. And those who've done it will attest that it's quite a blast to boot.

This book's intent is to immerse you in the world of theater festivals of new work, to give you an inside glimpse at how the fest scene operates, and to show you how to make it work for you. In a nutshell, what you hold in your hands is the theater pro's bible for navigating this world and coming out unscathed on the other side. Because despite the riches of potential payoffs, there are dangers lurking on the festival scene: artistic dangers, financial dangers, critical reception dangers, even physical dangers. Not to sound like your mom, but you gotta be careful when talking to strangers, especially at that solo performance festival you've somehow gotten stranded at in a muddy cow pasture in Scotland, with nothing left to your name except one measly Euro and the last three bites of a stale Toblerone bar. The first rule of the festival world: Prepare and plan before you dip a single toe in.

To that end, the first thing you must understand is that the main way a well-established, well-run festival benefits its artists is through the philosophy of volume. A gigantic gathering like the Edinburgh Festival Fringe draws thousands upon thousands to watch an average of 1,500 performances a year, and although many marginal shows may fall through the cracks, mass word of mouth routinely makes strong work successful. Even smaller-scale fests draw big audience numbers (certainly the ones listed in this book do, but we'll get to that shortly), and repeat festival-goers will really get behind a good show, see it numerous times, and bring in other folks to check it out. If you're an artist who is justifiably confident about the material you'll be presenting, and if you choose the right venue, you really can't go wrong.

How you CAN go wrong is by skipping the preliminary essentials. You've got to research festivals inside and out to select the ones to approach smartly, or you're sunk. You've got to hone and polish and perfect the work you want to do until it's absolutely as good as you can make it. You've got to brush up on your office skills: filling out applications, keeping track of deadlines, budgeting fees and travel expenses, and feasibly scheduling your road trips take discipline. You've got to pay attention to the practical: You need to pack right, know where you're going to sleep each night, know how to manage the production personnel you may be traveling with, and make sure you've got all your shots (literally). You've got to develop a tough hide and an outgoing personality if you don't already have both, because a huge component to successful "festing" is being able to sell yourself and your work.

In short, you need brains, resources, and chutzpah. If you've already got 'em, great. If not, this book will strive to arm you with 'em. I've structured it largely as a highly detailed, practical directory of sixty of the world's best festivals of new works (plus twenty-five honorable mentions). Of course, there are many, many more festivals around that showcase quality work, and I only wish I could have included scores more. I chose the specific fests I've included because I felt they had the playmakers' best interests covered: Their key personnel truly like and respect artists; their reputations are stellar; many are open to artists who are just emerging (and the grand old dames among them will give you places to learn from and aspire to); plus, they're set up to give you exposure and often good profits and benefits. Selected festivals are broken into three distinct categories, as well: fringe, performance-driven, and playwrights-focused.

The top sixty fests listed, in no particular order:

1. Edinburgh Festival Fringe, Scotland
2. Lincoln Center Festival
3. The John F. Kennedy Center's New Visions, New Voices Festival
4. BAM Next Wave Festival (Brooklyn Academy of Music)
5. NY International Fringe Festival
6. Ensemble Studio Theatre One-Act Marathon
7. Spoleto Festival USA
8. Piccolo Spoleto
9. Bay Area Playwrights' Festival
10. Hip-Hop Theater Festivals (NY and San Francisco)
11. Montreal Fringe, Canada
12. Dublin Fringe, Ireland
13. Dublin Theatre Festival, Ireland
14. Prague Fringe, Czech Republic
15. Moving Arts Premiere One-Act Competition/Festival
16. Minnesota Fringe
17. The Playwrights' Center Playlabs Festival
18. Trustus Playwrights' Festival
19. Rainbow Theatre Festival
20. Orlando Fringe
21. New Perspectives Theatre Company's Voices from the Edge Festival
22. EdgeFest
23. Ko Fest

24. Winnipeg Fringe, Canada

25. Ottawa Fringe, Canada

26. Edmonton Fringe, Canada

27. Toronto Fringe, Canada

28. Adelaide Fringe, Australia

29. Rhinoceros Theater Festival

30. World's Quickest Theater Festival (14/48)

31. Seattle Festival of Improv Theatre

32. Midtown International Theatre Festival

33. Vital Signs Festival

34. Attic Theatre One-Act Marathon

35. TheatreWorks New Works Festival

36. (Perishable Theatre) Women Playwrights' Festival

37. San Francisco Fringe

38. Short Attention Span PlayFEST

39. Contemporary American Theatre Festival

40. Boston Theatre Marathon

41. Belfast Festival, Ireland

42. Victoria Fringe/Uno Festival of Solo Performance, Canada

43. Philadelphia Fringe

44. Baltimore Playwrights' Festival

45. Coe College Playwriting Festival

46. Vancouver Fringe, Canada

47. National Audio Theatre Festivals

48. Genesius Guild events

49. National Alliance for Musical Theatre New Works Festival

50. Humana Festival of New American Plays (Actors' Theatre of Louisville).

51. Festival of Autumn (Festival D'Automne), France

52. Israel Festival, Israel

53. Caracas International Theatre Festival, Venezuela

54. International Istanbul Theatre Festival, Turkey

55. Viladecans International Theatre and Animation Festival, Spain

56. Göteberg Dance and Theatre Festival, Sweden

The book's additional chapters will hopefully serve you as an experience-driven advice guide. A wide variety of festival movers and shakers have been generous enough to share their opinions, experiences, and unvarnished truths with regard to the fringe scene, and their words are worth their weight in gold. On the one hand, you're getting the wisdom of a Paul Gudgin, who heads up Edinburgh, or a Nigel Redden, the director of both the Spoleto USA and Lincoln Center fest; on the other hand, veteran performers who live their lives traveling the circuit are giving you a bird's-eye, slice-of-life viewpoint. This is the real score, plain and simple, and taking in these professionals' sage advice will give you a major leg up. I've also packed this book to the brim with key nuts-and-bolts information: how to tell whether a festival is right for you by asking the right questions, how the creative process happens in a festival context, a full business primer, the skinny on festival lifestyle issues, and lots more. You'll take a fun and fascinating festival history lesson, see how that history evolved to shape today's festival world, hear some juicy war stories, and hopefully, by the end, feel ready, willing, and eager to enter the scene to convey your own creative message as you ideally wish to express it. Read on, and get inspired.

PART 1 The

Essentials

1

In the Beginning

It's 1947, and the world of theater is about to change forever—for the better.

Architects of the Revolution

Eight radical bands of playmakers plant themselves at the gates of the well-respected Edinburgh Festival in Scotland. They're ready to wow the festival's capacity crowds with their respective brands of creative genius—except there's just one little catch. There's no room for these merry bands to perform on the festival's schedule.

Undaunted, our thespians trudge over to some of the more distant festival stages, away from the big audiences and the festival leaders who've turned them down. And boom—they just start performing. They get on with things without the benefit of PR, an operating, centrally located box office, anything. Slowly but surely, word starts to spread that these ragtag radicals are really good, and people start filling their makeshift houses.

A year later, Robert Kemp, a writer for the *Evening News*, heartily endorsed a repeat engagement by these playmakers. Without intending to, he also came up with the official name of a legend-in-the-making when he used the phrase "fringe" to describe the edgy outskirts upon which these artists were working. Not long after, Edinburgh University students started putting up the "fringers" in their dorms so the show could go on.

As the fringe festival grew in notoriety, it grew in scope, and tons of would-be fringers descended on Edinburgh. Not surprisingly, jealousy and competition reared its ugly head; sure, there was room for everybody to perform, but arguments got pretty savage when it came to the fair way to organize and split up the now-sizable box-office profit pie. By 1954, conditions had deteriorated to the point that all of the participating fringe groups knew there was nothing left to do but give in and cooperate with each other. They met, and worked out feasible solutions for managing money *and* publicity. By the next year, Edinburgh University students were managing not only the fringe box office, but a fringe café as well. The Edinburgh Festival Fringe was essentially born at this point (and was actually getting pretty professional pretty quickly). In 1958, its constitution became official: The main point of this charter was the vow that there would be absolutely no judgments, vetting, or limits placed on any artist's work within the festival.

The Path of Progress

As a few more years pass, the Fringe became plagued by growing pains. Participating companies expanded from thirteen per fest to nineteen per fest to twenty-eight per fest, to a record thirty-four companies by 1962. Venue space was getting tight, and the students trying to run everything effectively started to get a bit overwhelmed. Volunteers attempted to pick up the slack, but because business was routinely run out of people's flats, things started getting crazy quickly. Time to rethink things. By 1969, the Fringe was successfully re-launched as a limited company, under the guidance of chairman Lord Grant. Now the festival was eligible for public funding, and an office was established.

Enter John Milligan. He joined the Fringe as its first administrator in 1971, and swiftly took steps to further organize the festival's business. An awards program was instituted the following year; also, in '72, the Fringe showcased an incredible forty-five new plays. Growth continued at a fast clip under new Fringe administrator Alistair Moffat, and by the end of the seventies, almost five hundred groups were performing per Fringe.

By the early eighties, Fringe venues had been established all over Edinburgh, including the festival's now-famous "super-venues"—mega-houses Gilded Balloon, the Assembly Rooms, and Pleasance. Michael Dale and Mhairi Mackenzie-Robinson followed Moffat into the administrator's chair, and the Fringe started fundraising madly. Things got pretty spiffy—the fest took up residence in custom-designed offices on Edinburgh's High Street, a new computer system brought the fest into the nineties in state-of-the-art fashion, and over a thousand companies routinely performed per fest.

The Movement Spreads

Still, despite all of this progress, all of these upgrades, and all of the innovation, something never changed: the Fringe's dogged devotion to its original mission. In the mid-nineties, some folks within the Fringe inner circle started getting up in arms about the sheer influx of performers hurling themselves into the festival, and major consideration was given to limiting the number of participants. This period of self-doubt was vanquished pretty much single-handedly by Hilary Strong, the Fringe's new director, who came aboard in 1994. She refuses to budge from the idea of unfettered creativity that the fest was founded on—artistic freedom survives and thrives here, and ultimately, so do a record 1,500-plus Fringe presentations.

As the Edinburgh Fringe was exploding, not unexpectedly, additional fests started to crop up all over Europe and even in some parts of Latin America. An "informal revue" movement of fests was being organized by such folks in the UK as Dudley Moore and Tom Stoppard. By the seventies, it became quite conceivable to tour a "circuit" of such festivals, and if you could talk a good game and get people into your show, you could actually make a good living as an actor, writer, or director. In many ways, this period of time can be considered the "golden age" for festivals abroad. Long-established festivals took note of the new creative charge in the air, and programming at festivals everywhere became more vibrant and important than ever. Opines Stella Hall, director of the highly regarded Belfast Festival at Queen's University in Ireland, says, "I think if you look at some of the successes in the festival in terms of the local work that was being presented, it's work that spoke very much to the Irish condition—both work presented onstage at professional theaters like the Lyric Theatre, and work being produced by independent companies like Tinderbox. [That's true even today.] But also, there is a very, very vibrant community theater movement in Belfast."

This new method of theatrical expression started to truly go global during the decade before, in 1982. In Edmonton, Canada, artists were watching the inroads being made in Europe (Edinburgh especially) with great interest. The Edmonton Fringe's establishment in '82 was marked by a similar commitment to artistic freedom and to the Fringe patron (who, organizers believed, should be able to take in as many performances as possible—so ticket prices had to stay low).

Edmonton also wanted to attract as diverse a cross-section of work as possible. This led to flashes of dramatic brilliance—and also to crash-and-burn mega-bombs. No matter! The whole point of this fringe, or of any open fringe anywhere in the world, is, admirably, democracy. Edmonton started drawing very big crowds—at times, big, noisy, eccentric crowds—and earned the rep of being one of the best times you could possibly have on Canadian soil.

Fringe festivals started to pop up all over Canada—from Vancouver to Toronto to Ottawa and beyond. The movement became so widespread that in 1984, the Canadian Association of Fringe Festivals (CAFF) was founded in order to provide organization and support to member festivals. The United States started to sprout fringes as well—in Seattle, Orlando, Florida, San Francisco, Minneapolis, and more cities. (A number of U.S. Fringes joined CAFF as well.) Add those free-form fests to the list of more traditional performance, playwrights', general arts, and educational festivals across North America, and it's clear how much artistic and financial opportunity truly exists within the framework of this world.

The Success Story

Flash-forward to today. TJ Dawe is one of the North American festival circuit's most famous and dynamic performers. He's nick-named the "King of the Fringe." Festival leaders speak glowingly of him from coast to coast in Canada and the United States; his fellow performers watch in awe as he demonstrates total command of his audience. He stands onstage alone, speaking to the audience of his experiences in the real world; he directs groundbreaking versions of the movies he adored as a kid. Here's his story:

"I grew up wanting to be an actor. As a kid, I saw the kind of peak period of the movies by Steven Spielberg and George Lucas. I was three or four when I saw *Star Wars*. *Raiders of the Lost Ark*, *E.T.*—movies like that took me out of myself and made me in love with that world of stories, and I wanted to be involved with that. I wanted to be an actor, but I didn't see much theater; growing up in Vancouver, there isn't that much. I mean, there's some, but how much does a kid see? Just stuff that comes to your school. Like most kids, I watched a lot more movies and watched a lot more TV than I saw plays.

"After high school, I went to the University of Victoria to study acting, because I'd heard they had a really good theater department. While I was there, it was a tough go—a lot of people there had been stars of their high school drama class, and I was one of them, and suddenly you get there and you're no one. You're not getting cast, you're not getting lead roles, and you're not sure if your dreams are gonna come true. At the end of my second year there, I'd only played one role in two years.

"One of the grad students was auditioning for a play he was going to tour across the Canadian Fringe circuit. Now, my high school, coincidentally, had been on the same block as the Vancouver Fringe, but I'd never even seen one play there— I didn't even know it was a theater festival. I didn't want to have anything to do with it—it seemed like a really weird festival, it was in kind of a shady part of town, and there were these weird posters that were up around the beginning of school every year, and weird people in the neighborhood. I didn't even want to go near it. So anyway, I just auditioned for this, because like any actor, you audition for anything you can. It was a play called *Never Swim Alone*. When I read the script for this one, I wanted more than anything to be in it, and I ended up getting the part.

"We rehearsed in May 1994, and in mid-June we hit the road I was nineteen years old. We played in Toronto, Winnipeg, Saskatoon, and Victoria. I was a hired actor—I didn't administrate the tour, I didn't put up any of the money. I performed the show, I put up posters, and I handed out flyers to line-ups. It really opened my eyes to what the Canadian fringe circuit was. It was still pretty new for that point—I think for only about five years had there been a circuit that someone could possibly tour from east to west, and the director had done that the year before. I just wanted to be in a good play. The thought of touring was exciting and romantic because I'd never toured—I didn't realize how hard it is. How much struggling and starvation is involved.

"The show was an artistic success. It was a wonderful play to be involved in, and it got some good reviews and good houses, even though we made no money. So for the next year at school, I just starved—I think I made $400 for a full summer's work. I continued studying acting—it was kind of up and down. I was a good actor, but not a great one, still never cast often, so I had a lot of energy and nothing to do with it. So I started writing. One of the summers home from the university, I bought a typewriter. I was working a truck-driving job that summer, and I was staying at my parents' house deep in the 'burbs—there was no cultural life, there was nowhere to go after work. I just bought this electric typewriter, and would come home and just write—write about anything that had been in my mind. I just kept doing that—when I got back to university I kept on writing, and eventually formulated the desire to write a one-man show. I had no idea how to write plays. I had no training as a writer, never wanted to be a writer, never thought of myself as a writer, even though while at university I became a voracious reader, mostly of novels, not plays. I wanted to perform, so I wanted to write and perform.

"After my final year of university, I wrote a one-man show. I couldn't get a job; I was living in a basement suite, I was on welfare, and just spending my time at the typewriter and reading. I put on my first one-man show in my old theater department and it went really well, so the next September, I wrote my second one-man show and put it on in my first fringe, which was the Victoria Fringe, in 1997, and then wrote another one, and toured that across Canada. That third show, called *Tired Clichés*, was the first one that was a real artistic success, where I really felt I had something good. It got great reviews all across the country and made decent money. I'd already been on the fringe circuit once, so I had a good idea what these cities were.

"If I hadn't done that, if I hadn't been in that show when I was nineteen, I probably wouldn't have thought of the fringe circuit as this viable place to put on plays. At these festivals, people were looking for new theater. They were looking for something experimental and accessible and hopefully funny, although it doesn't have to be. Most of the plays put on at a fringe are unpublished, never will be published, and probably will never be performed again. In most theater worlds, that's the last kind of stuff people want to see, whereas on the fringe, that's *exactly* what people want to see. Most theater patrons want to see something they know—they wanna see Shakespeare or *My Fair Lady*. But on the fringe, if you're gonna do Shakespeare, you'd better fuck with it. You'd better cross-cast it or set it on a fire escape or turn it into a one-man show; otherwise, you're not gonna hold people's attention.

"As I toured, I got to develop my shows. I guess I had a writer's voice in me the whole time, but as a theater student you're not taught to ad-lib. If anything, that's the last thing you're supposed to do onstage; the words are sacred. But if it was my own script, I could. I didn't have a director there, either—there was no one there, it was just me, so if a line came to me, I would just throw it in. This became an essential part of my process, too, and is still is. My shows are always fifteen minutes longer by the time I've reached the west coast than when I premiere them on the east coast.

"On the fringe circuit, I get to do about forty or fifty performances in a tour. I'm not really based out of Vancouver or Toronto—I don't so much have a home, I'm not part of a theater community anywhere, and one of the things that's kind of disenchanting to me about the thought of being part of these communities is that I'll see people in Vancouver who get grant funding and put on a show, run for a week or two, and that's it. Maybe a year later, they'll put it on again in some other theater in some other town, and then they'll do seven more perform- ances. It's like, that's nothing! I really get to explore the material with fifty performances and different audiences across the coun- try. And to make money on top of all of that! In the last three years, I've started to make my living at this, so at this point, it's starting to pay really well. For my first three years, I was taking a day job in the off-season to pay the rent, because you also have to pay money to do these tours. You have to pay about five hundred dollars a city for the fee, and you have to get yourself there, and the money for posters and flyers and photos and press kits and postage and food while you're on the road—none of it's cheap. So it's difficult to do. But I am a one-man operation, so I have no one else to pay—but no one else to share the work.

"It's probably the easiest way to self-produce theater, because they find the venue for you. And you're part of a festival context, so the press is automatically interested and the audience is auto- matically interested—in the festival, though not necessarily in you. It's still not absolutely easy—I had no experience as a pub- licist, as a producer, anything—and I just learned how to do it. The Fringe will give you forms, and walk you through how to do a press release if you've never done one before. And you see what works and doesn't work, and while you're touring, you talk to other performers about how they're doing it. Everyone's trying to be original. Everyone's trying to do something nobody else has, and yet be accessible, because everyone wants an audi- ence and the only money you make is your box office. So you see people take wild chances in a way that they just can't when the stakes are a lot higher, when the superstructure's a lot higher, when there are a lot more people involved.

"There's no filter between me and the audience, me and what I want to say. I don't have to go through an editor or a board of directors or anything like that. It's entirely what I want to do, and in terms of writing and putting on a play, it's instant gratification. I can have an idea, and six months later, I'm performing it."

How the Past Informs the Future

Dawe's story perfectly encompasses the way festival history has come full circle to inform and influence today's festival world: It's all about creating opportunity. Had those daring thesps back in '47 not had the nerve to take control and invent their own mode of performance, today's festival journeymen would never get a single shot.

The festival world only works for self-starters. The huge burden of responsibility for yourself you must assume on the scene scares off many artists, and well it should: Wallflowers need not apply. You need to look after yourself and your survival—artistically, financially, and physically—before you can truly be any good to a company you're collaborating with, or for a producer who might dig your work. You have to have eyes in the back of your head, be willing to take a bath in a stream in the dead of night if necessary, make sure you don't get sick or lose too much weight or tick off the head of one fest by being late because you were having too good a time at another fest. You have to be a grownup to do well—but if you have such a mature attitude, the only limits you'll face will be largely self-imposed. If the play you've written is terrific, if your performance style is fresh, and if the monologue you're directing is solid, it matters as well. Why? Because the festival world is set up to reward the worthy individual.

The most desired commodity to be found in the work at any festival today, as in the beginning, is originality. How many other forms of art can you say that about in today's crassly safe commercial world? Things just get more and more outrageously fresh as the years pass, too, so that the most out-there stuff is now actually considered the norm. In fact, artistic power brokers on today's fest scene actively compete with each other for the most exciting, outrageous, and artistically significant pieces of work. Artists are actually praised and rewarded in the fest world for aggressively pushing the envelope. How refreshing. Want to be part of it? Our first step will be to arm you with specifics, logistics, and a grasp of how the entire fest paradigm works, top to bottom.

2

Learning the Ropes

Theater festivals come in so many different versions, varieties, and themes that you'd get absolutely dizzy trying to sort them out yourself on a worldwide scope. The great thing about such incredible diversity, of course, is that somewhere, there's going to be a fest (or twenty-seven) that's right for your work. The tough part is hunting the appropriate forums down.

What can be extraordinarily helpful when it comes to differentiating between fests is understanding the way the entire festival scene works from the inside. There are commonly known and very distinct categories of festivals, to start with. A basic grasp of these groupings, and how they respectively function, will start you on the road toward hooking up with the best fests for you. So let's start learning. This chapter will kick off with a comprehensive discussion of the various types of new works festivals. We'll go on to cover the hugely important issue of research—the right way to analyze whether a particular fest might be receptive to your particular kind of work, just for starters. So much of the success you may enjoy on the scene is actually determined before you ever leave home—that's right, planning is nearly everything. You want to do it accurately; you don't want to waste time and energy, which you're going to need on the road later. In a nutshell, knowing everything you can in advance about the fests you want to approach will give you much more confidence when it comes time to actually approach them.

The Big Breakdown

Theater festivals essentially fall into one of the following classifications.

Festivals That Are Simply Festive

There are scores of theatrical venues that dub themselves "festivals" and celebrate a certain playwright, or programmed season. These organizations often produce works that are truly glorious, but they remain outside the scope of this book. The venerated Oregon Shakespeare Festival and the Shaw Festival are two examples. These are established theaters or theater companies whose name contains the word "festival," but who do not necessarily focus on new work, or the self-created work of diverse performers.

Some established fests listed within these pages may seem to contradict this policy at first. For instance, the Humana Festival of New American Plays is actually part of the programming of the regional theater the Actor's Theatre of Louisville. Still, Humana crosses over perfectly because its major thrust is on brand-new material. Our focus in this book is on fests that carry forward the trailblazing traditions established by the first Edinburgh Fringe. Although many festive fests produce wonderfully innovative productions, it's got to be wholly original stuff to play in our ballpark.

Fringe Festivals

Many fests that term themselves "fringe" operate under the founding principles of the movement laid out in chapter 1. They put no artistic limitations on playmakers, never censor so much as a comma of written or performed material, and have no "quality" criteria—really amazing shows can share stage time with stupefyingly awful shows. These fests are called "unjuried," and often accept applications/submissions from would-be participants via a lottery or first-come, first-served basis only, to ensure there's absolutely no favoritism, and to loosely ensure some cap in terms of the sheer number of shows on a single program. Despite this attempt to avoid being overrun by too many companies, unjuried fringe festivals often stage hundreds, if not over a thousand, shows at a time.

A second sub-group of fringe fests are termed "curated" or "juried." A curated fringe does impose selection criteria to a certain extent within its programming process. How this might happen, for instance: The fest's artistic director sees a young Sarah Jones working her performance magic in a tiny, airless basement space somewhere downtown in New York, and invites her to perform at his fringe—but puts no limits on the actual elements of her artistic statement at the fringe. There's actually quite a bit of tension within the fringe ranks in regard to unjuried-versus-curated mode of operation. Nick Stucchio of the Philadelphia Fringe has been on both side of the fence. "There's this fringe movement going around the world, and much of the movement claims that the fringe movement is fundamentally about non-juration," he says. "The movement is a reaction to people like me, who do curate. There's a North American Association of Fringe Festivals, and they sort of build in that philosophy against juration. Although I think that the conditions for the fringe festival are now changing rapidly, and I think it's a time in this culture of choice to continually mount something like that."

So are artists penalized or discriminated against if they choose to work first at an unjuried fringe, and then later at a juried fringe? Absolutely not. Although both sides of the movement may differ in the approach they take to programming, any good fringe director or producer, juried or unjuried, will tell you he or she supports all artists, period. The choice of which type of fringe to present at rests solely with the playmaker. Many playmakers jump back and forth between unjuried and juried at every stage of their career, too.

From an artist's viewpoint, is an unjuried fringe preferable to a curated fringe, or vice versa? It depends on what you're after. Unjuried fringes offer you the chance to soar creatively, but you can't really count on any form of stability profit-wise, because competition is just too stiff among the scores of shows programmed together. A curated fringe may be tougher to gain entry to, but often artists can work out a favorable monetary deal with the organization, as there are fewer shows pro-grammed into a single festival.

Unjuried or curated, a huge advantage that fringe festivals offer playmakers is the chance to have their work discovered. "What we do best is we act as much as possible as a sort of dating agency," says Edinburgh Fringe director Paul Gudgin. "We put on the festival and give the platform for these fantastic performers and plays to take place. Then what we try to do is encourage as many promoters and directors and theater producers to come to Edinburgh to see them as possible. We don't specifically send them to see any particular plays. What we avoid doing is making judgments and choices. What we do is if a theater director comes to us and says he's looking for this particular type of work, or that particular type of work, is we'll help him find it. Or we will pass on the benefit of anything we've got or anything we've heard—if someone says they're looking for new writing, we'll say, 'Well, actually, we have heard that this is a particularly good show.'

"What we do is enable. We help them get the tickets; we help them find shows they might be particularly interested in. But after that, we leave them to get together. We might help them get together, but whether that turns into a blossoming marriage or a frosty relationship is then up to them.

"Sometimes it would be nice to sort of be involved with projects that go on to the next level, but we don't view that as our role. Our role is to give them the platform of the festival to put their event on, and to try and bring these parties together, but then we leave them, if you will, to do the rest of the business themselves."

David Fuller, Artistic Director of the Jean Cocteau Repertory in New York, has in recent years taken a keen interest in the fest scene as part of his other life—as a respected theater critic covering the New York Fringe. "I'm astounded now by the worldwide interest in the fringe scene," he marvels. "I think it's amazing, the broad range of performances brought to the festival. This year, on one end of the spectrum I saw a musical comedy called *The Passion of George W. Bush*, and on the other, a play produced by the Epic Theatre Company, written by an Indian playwright, with supertitles."

He also lauds the fact that despite the subsequent Broadway triumph of this fringe's former offering—*Urinetown*—productions have not become obviously commercialized. "I think the leadership of the New York Fringe has been very careful—not saying 'no' to possibly commercial shows, but on the other hand, there are a great deal of shows being done that just will never be seen in that way, and that's a very good thing."

Another huge advantage to working at a fringe is the ability it affords you to make work with relative ease. Most theater artists know what a colossal headache hunting down spaces, dealing with tech issues, and scrambling to lure an audience is. At a fringe, such basics are already covered, allowing you to focus on your work. Shannan Calcutt, a veteran fringe performer who has toured her clown character Izzy in three separate shows on the circuit, explains, "You can go to a fringe festival and pay five hundred dollars or six hundred dollars and have six shows with a front-of-house manager, with box office, with a festival technician, and with a festival that's advertised and promoted. So people are coming to your show—that's an amazing gift right there.

It's a different audience as well. Particularly with some of the Canadian festivals, it's a very smart audience. They've gone to the fringe for years, they know experimental theatre with an edge. So you're playing to a sophisticated audience as well, which is fantastic when you want feedback on your material. I've found the fringe fantastic on that—you just sort of get word-of-mouth building from city to city. It's a fantastic place to get reviewed, because again, the press is coming; you just have to get them into your show."

Performance-Driven Festivals

The craft of the actor and his contribution to new work is celebrated at this kind of fest. There are many strong improv festivals in North America, the UK, and Australia, for example. Solo performance festivals are a dominant current trend, cropping up frequently in recent years all over the United States and Canada.

Actors tend to gravitate toward performance festivals for two very disparate but equally valid reasons: Either they want the chance to break out and bravely shine on their own, or they want a new performance adventure within the safe confines of a company collaboration. In the latter case, you can easily transplant the well-oiled-machine aspect of a group that's used to developing work together into the freshness of a fest environment. Bringing that group sensibility to a festival can win a good company many new fans and lots of attention.

Another hallmark of the performance-driven festival is often community influence. I'm not talking about a summer stock–loving retirement community. Not that the umpteenth production of *Kiss Me, Kate* can't be a winner; it's just not what we're focused on here. Indeed, performance fests offering new works sometimes program to be friendly to the locals, a point to keep in mind when evaluating whether your work might fit into a specific fest's context. Nigel Redden, Spoleto USA director, stresses how important community involvement with a festival truly is in terms of shaping its artistic fingerprints: "That sense of trying to make Charleston

(South Carolina) a focal point part of what the festival was, I think has become essential for festivals, so that one doesn't become simply a festival that could be done in Charleston, or could be done in New York, or could be done in Aspen, or could be done in Santa Fe. Somehow, the place has to inform the festival in some deep and fundamental fashion. That has been a fascinating aspect of the festival."

Performance-driven festivals are often cross-pollinated with other art forms, which may include dance, music, multimedia, or performance art facets in addition to theater. Some festivals end up an eclectic mess when programmed this way; others, like Spoleto or the Lincoln Center Festival, obviously sing like a bird. As a rule, the better attended a multi-genre performance fest is, the better organized it's going to be, and the more it's worth your time. And . . .

The harder it's going to be to get into the more prestigious ones. Only the most naïve playmaker walking among us believes that her homemade, shaky camcorder-shot performance video is gonna knock Laurie Anderson right out of a prime slot at BAM Next Wave. Not to say that confidence won't take you far; there are just more practical ways to consider which festivals your performance work belongs in, and how to maneuver your entry. A few examples:

• The best way to get your improv team into a respected improvisation festival is through live performance, if possible. You want a representative or scout from that fest to see you working on your feet, with a live audience that's truly getting off on your performance as you create it. (This is, obviously, the whole nature of the improv beast.) Call, write, or e-mail the fest you're targeting to invite its personnel to a club show you've booked that's geographically close TO THEM. That may mean traveling to play a gig in a distant city. If so, inconvenience yourself, and do it. You want to make coming to check out your stuff as easy as possible for the fest folks you really want to work for.

- Middle-range performance fests often like to see live auditions at their headquarters. Sometimes these are booked through casting agents; sometimes, you can finagle such a go-see by sending in a resume, photo, and cover letter describing the original work you do. It can't hurt to inquire—preferably by mail or e-mail—how the fest you're interested in prefers to learn about its talent.

- Attracting attention (and maybe, MAYBE) a slot at one of the big guns (like Lincoln Center or Spoleto) happens when you've got three things going for you: heart, prestige, and testimony. In regard to heart: If you're doing fantastic work that's garnering favorable press from very reputable print outlets (like great reviews from major city newspapers or national magazines), by all means, package up a performance tape with those write-ups and send it in. In regard to prestige: Make sure you've built a track record performing your original work at known and respected venues (like regional theaters) before you try to gain entry to a heavy-duty festival. The fest will want to make sure it can market your experience favorably, and the more lauded venues there are on your resume, the better. In regard to testimony: Nepotism does count (sometimes). Or at least solid endorsement does. If your mentor and favorite theater professor from college knows the head of a fest you covet, by all means, ask him to make a phone call on your behalf. Any connection you have who can vouch for your talent and professionalism can conceivably get your foot in the door.

Playwrights' Festivals

These fests often go above and beyond the call of duty in terms of simply showcasing material—they frequently serve as an invaluable refuge where a playwright can actually develop her work in a performance setting. Kim Peter Kovac, senior program director of youth and family programs at the John F. Kennedy Center, speaks to the value of developmental festivals by retelling the origins of the highly esteemed New Visions/New Voices fest: "The original impetus for New Visions came out of conversations about new plays, especially challenging, daring ones . . . wanting to find an opportunity to hear them, know a little bit about them. Then the concept evolved into being more about brand-new plays, and involving other theaters.

"From the beginning, a few key ideas were in place: (A) theater-driven (in terms of being collaborative), not entirely playwright-driven; (B) plays at any stage of development. One of the plays selected for the first New Visions was David Saar's *The Yellow Boat*, a co-production of Childsplay in Tempe, Arizona, and Metro Theater in St. Louis. We knew that David Saar was having trouble getting started on the play, quite probably because it was about his son, who had quite recently died of pediatric AIDS. I remember being at a conference with David, when he said that he didn't have much written. I said that (A) he had to come to the festival because his play was in the brochure and (B) it didn't matter how much he wrote before the festival—that it was all about process. Actually, not one word of the script had been written before New Visions. David had written a prose, short story version; we found five actors good at improvisation, and they began crafting the play right there. We've often had first drafts that were hot off the Xerox five minutes before the first rehearsal. Last New Visions, at least one script was finished at New Visions, with the writer coming in with about half of it at the beginning. So, from the beginning, the idea that scripts could be at any stage of development was cemented."

The collaborative nature of these playwrights' festivals can be extremely nurturing to playwrights, and in fact may lead to long-term, recurrent relationships between the writer and the festival producer. "I see this over and over in our work in the theater—that the teams of people who work together often develop more quickly a strong language of theater, and a more personal language," observes Charles Fee, esteemed artistic director of the Idaho Shakespeare and Great Lakes Theatre festivals. "You see this with playwrights regularly. When we look at many great play-wrights, we realize that one of the things that was helpful to them in their early careers was working in a given theater space with a given acting company, and with what feel like constrictions on their work by the space, by the actors, by the directors. But in fact, what it allows them to do is to develop a very deep sensibility."

Playwrights' festivals sometimes work as contests or competi-tions, where submissions are accepted and read, finalists are chosen, and one or more of those finalist plays gets a production within a fest (and usually a cash prize or stipend). Other times, a festival will shepherd a good piece of work through development and a world premiere in hopes of catching the eye of another production entity, to achieve a commercial pick-up. The festival then may or may not maintain a stake in any future profits the play/playwright might earn; that's negotiable. Zan Sawyer-Dailey of Actors Theatre of Louisville comments in regard to Humana: "We're constantly, con-stantly reading. We go to all of the other playwrights' festivals, so we can not only see the work, but also continuously meet people, and continuously learn about people coming in to the field. Our goal continues to be to find the most interesting plays we can. It's a pretty rugged process to narrow the field down to six each year.

"One of our general goals is to find work that will move in to the national literature. We do site-specific work; we do work that is probably a one-time-only event. But that is not our norm; our norm is to do things that will then move into general circulation and the American literature, but also create careers for these playwrights. You look at somebody like David Rambo, whose play *God's Man in Texas* we did a couple of years ago; it's a very nifty little well-made play about a very specific storyline. It's just a terrific piece for three actors. It has been produced everywhere; it has made David Rambo a regional theater name. That's a great success story for us.

"For many, many, many years, it has not been our goal to get these works into New York. A lot of them do go to New York, but we do not have a proprietary interest in these plays. What we do is we introduce these playwrights to the national press, and they get a tremendous mount of visibility." Humana hosts the national and international press on the culminating weekends of the festival, and on its first weekend, hosts distinguished artistic personnel, all in an effort to showcase great work.

Targeting Your Turf

Once you've determined which general type of fest category your work seems to fit into, it's time to laser-beam in which precise fests to approach. So how, and where, to start? It's important to focus on the following points.

Size and Scope

Which festivals draw the biggest audiences? This is a vital piece of information to have, because it's a real either/or. Either you want to go with a gigantic gathering with as wide a demographic as possible because you feel strongly that your work is ready to rock, or you want to start off slowly, under the radar. Your gut will immediately tell you where you're at on this, so listen to it.

For the most up-to-date info on current audience demographics (which fluctuate wildly), head straight to the Web site of a festival you're interested in. And don't just use that Web site to answer one question for yourself—study it from top to bottom to learn absolutely everything you can about a fest you're serious about pursuing. It's remarkable how often artists actually call in or submit to festivals with no clue whatsoever about what that festival actually programs, and who it programs for. Fergus Linehan, director of the Dublin Theatre Festival in Ireland, stresses the importance of basic research: "Endless homework. Actually, a lot of people do kind of call you up, and you go, 'Did you ever even go to our Web site?' Classically, they sort of ring up and they say, 'I'm doing a piece—it's a one-person show based on the life of George Bernard Shaw. I did it in the university last year—it got a great reception!' And you're going, 'We have a five-hundred-seat theatre to fill!'

"If you do study our Web site, you'll see that we have a lot of things going on around the edges of our festival. We have a children's season, we have a program of new European writing and translation. So there's all of those things going on as well. If you really know an event, you're more likely to be able to ask intelligent questions about it."

Write to a festival and ask for brochures, an information packet, anything you can get. Most fests are really cool about sending potential contributors as much material as they have available. But don't waste a festival office's time with dopey phone calls. The phone, you know, is rarely the best way to make a good professional first impression. Submit a complete application and all essential supplementary materials to a fest by mail instead. Such a package looks polished and complete. If you have questions after that, I *still* would be very careful about calling, especially if those questions are in regard to your prospects of being selected. It's so much classier to be chased rather than to chase.

The Word on the Street

In a perfect world, you could quit your day job and fly across the globe, immersing yourself in the sights and sounds of every fest that struck your fancy. That's probably not too practical, though. Ideally, you should attend any festival you want to work at that's within reasonable radius, but if you can't, reading up on the opinion of others is the next best thing to being there. Google a fest and check out its reviews, any blog dirt you might be able to pick up, whatever you can find. You shouldn't believe everything you read (especially on the Web), but if a fest consistently racks up the same kind of comments—like they're slow to pay artists, for example—consider it a warning.

If you get the chance to chat up an actor, writer, or director who's worked at a festival you're interested in, jump at it. Ask this person about his/her experience with the tangible stuff (like how tough it was to apply, what tech conditions felt like within the actual space, etc.) but also with the subjective stuff (Were people there friendly? Cutthroat? Was the climate super-hot or super-cold? Any good, cheap restaurants in town?). Don't pry or drive your acquaintances crazy trolling for details. Just let them convey their enthusiasm (or distaste) about a fest to you organically: If someone has had a vivid experience somewhere, either positive or negative, he's probably going to want to express it.

A Track Record

Every theater insider knows the inspiring story behind *Urine-town* (mentioned earlier in the chapter), which started garnering attention at the New York International Fringe and ended up a Tony-winning Broadway triumph. As you can imagine, FringeNYC proudly toots its own horn whenever it can regarding this little musical that could, and rightly so. My point? Pay attention to what a festival touts as its high points, especially in promotional literature like brochures—it will tell you a lot about how strong a springboard that fest could offer for *your* production. A hit commercial transfer or two also indicates that producers who can actually get things accomplished check out a particular fest's offerings. The big-name festivals are obviously going to draw the moneymen with the deepest pockets—but not exclusively. Any Manhattan-based festival with a good reputation is geographically advantaged when it comes to option-hungry producers, and in Los Angeles, lots of movie folks check out new works fests in hopes of snapping up a piece or two that might work in the film medium.

What a Fest Wants

Knowing what specific challenges various festivals you target hope to meet in terms of expanding their own scope is key. Joseph Melillo, executive producer of the BAM Next Wave Festival, for instance, hopes to present "younger generations of artists from the USA and global community." A fact like this will breeze over the heads of nine out of ten potential festival applicants, because it seems like institutional planning, like it doesn't relate directly to the artist. But what could relate more directly to the artist than whether he or she is the prototype a festival wants to showcase?

Here's another instance in which reading festival promo materials pays off. Check out the most current statements in brochures, on Web sites, or in articles regarding a festival's plans for growth and expansion, or new artistic programs being developed. See where you might fit in terms of both a festival's intent and whether you're comfortable preserving work within this parameter.

Keeping Things Together

Print out any information about each festival you're researching that you find useful and relevant. Now get yourself a medium-sized metal or plastic file box with a handle for portability—good if you ultimately need to travel with this kind of information—and a box of hanging file folders. (Both can be had for a grand total of less than $20.) Organize each festival's material within its own file, adding in any promo stuff you've received, plus any notes you may have from conversations with artists who've worked at any of the fests. Keep your festival files alphabetized and in order at all times—this little stash of information is just going to grow and grow with time, and become more invaluable as you make connections and eventually secure actual performance berths. (Sooner or later, with a little hard work and luck, your data stash will swell so much you'll have to move on to an actual file cabinet).

Definitely collect more information that you think you can actually use, on more festivals than you conceivably think you could actually travel to. How come? Because within that stack of information, you may just find a kernel that could send your career in a whole new terrific direction. Maybe there's a reviewer's name buried within a festival file you might get to know later on. Maybe a magazine article on grant funding that makes no sense to you now will net you money in the future. You never know—so don't throw anything away.

Also, read and re-read everything you've hunted down and gathered. Become your own expert on each festival you're targeting. This will help you tremendously when filling out an application, or meeting face-to-face with a festival artistic or tech director—and those things definitely lie in your immediate future. The more time you spend studying a festival, the more smoothly and adroitly you'll be able to converse with those who matter within its parameters—and the more confident you'll become about your chances of actually becoming part of it.

3

Working the System

Once you've determined the type of festival that seems appropriate for your type of work, and have a target list of fests you'd love to approach in mind, it's time to actually start doing some approaching. What follows is everything you need to know to make your best impression, find out all the inside skinny about a fest you're interested in, and communicate smartly with fest personnel.

Advice from a Veteran

Charlie Ross is an old hand at festivals, having toured as a performer for well over a decade in multiple countries. Here he relates his history on the scene:

"There were four of us on my first tour, and it was rather expensive, really. Probably not as expensive on a large theatrical scale, like if you were doing a New York run or something, but for a bunch of students, it was rather expensive. It wasn't a big moneymaking venture; however, it was a great experience.

"It was a show called *Steam*—mediocre to good, but not really something you want to take on tour with four people. With four people, you can't expect to make much—I mean, you'll probably make your money back, which we did, but you won't actually make enough money to feel that you've had a job over the summer.

"I had university to pay for, so I ended up taking an acting job for nine years. It got a bit dull, because it was like a lunchbox acting job—like playing a cat in *Cats* for nine years. At some point you go, Oh, God, I have to get out of this.

The thing is, with fringe, it's an open book, forever. You can always do whatever you want, basically. There's really no limit to what you can do. So I had a sort of a quick, joking conversation with a friend: "Could you imagine seeing a one-person, three-minute version of Star Wars?" Three minutes seemed like a bit small to condense the film into, but what if you had to do that? What if you had to tell a story in three minutes, the whole thing?

Flash forward about six years. I was working on some radio plays. We had the opportunity to perform these radio plays in front of a small group of people, and we though, Why don't we take some of our other materials and also put those in front of people? It's a great opportunity to see what the audience thinks. So I wrote this one-person Star Wars. I didn't think it had any shelf value to it. I figured the thing would be pretty much a sketch—people might find it funny, and that would be pretty much the end of it. But there was really a strong reaction to it.

So I decided to basically put all my eggs into one basket. I gave up that job I'd had for nine years to try doing the Fringe again with this one-person venture. I have no costume, no set, no sound effects—it's the most portable show ever. It honestly could not have gone any better."

In 2003, Lucasfilm (the company owned by *Star Wars* creator George Lucas) came knocking on Ross's door. "It was such a fluke,"

Ross marvels. "I was down in Orlando doing *One-Man Star Wars*. I had a fifteen-minute conversation with Dan Roach, a stage producer from Chicago, who said, 'If you're ever interested in coming up to Chicago, you should give me a call.' We exchanged e-mail addresses, and I figured, maybe I'll hear from him, maybe not. He shot me a quick e-mail, I shot him one back, and by last fall, I was in Chicago doing the show for a couple of months. I got some great, high-profile reviews, and that managed to get Lucasfilm's attention. I wasn't sure if they were going to be angry, but they had actually heard good things about the show, and asked 'Can we see a video of it?' I said, 'Sure.'" This led to Ross being hired to perform at a live Lucasfilm event, the 2005 premiere of the final installment in the *Star Wars* saga.

Keeping his perspective practical has really helped Ross succeed. "I think you need to set realistic goals, or at the very least, not set such lofty goals that you're going to feel like you've failed," says Ross. "That doesn't mean limit your expectations; just don't have any expectations. Concentrate on the job at hand." A great philosophy—and you can make it work for you by combining it with a few smart strategies.

Be Honest with Yourself

"A lot of people quit after their first tour," says TJ Dawe. "A lot of people don't like the road; the poverty of your first tour is really, really trying, as well as the pressure of coming up with a new show immediately. And you have to start applying pretty much as soon as your tour is done. Right at the point of absolute exhaustion, and often when you're completely broke, you have to commit to a whole 'nother summer of touring. It really shapes your year."

Before you make a single move toward a single fest, sit down (with yourself if you're a solo performer or writer, or with your whole company if you're touring a show) and get real about where you truly are as a playmaker. Ask the following hard questions:

- Is my work truly ready for the rigors of a festival environment? Is it as polished and professional as I can make it? What are its obvious strengths? Weaknesses? Do its artistic pros outweigh its cons? (If not, it's time for reworking, not fest-going.)

- Am I financially capable of traveling with my show? Do I have money in an operating budget to carry me through time on the road, or do I have at least three months of personal savings I can use to finance the cost of a one-month trip? (Applying three times the cash you'll need to every month out ensures you've got an emergency reserve—don't leave home with less.)

- Do I have a daily budget worked out so I don't waste my precious resources?

- Have I planned the practicalities of where I'll sleep every night of the trip? (Inside someplace safe with doors and windows that lock is the only correct answer here. Thinking you can make do on a random bench in Central Park if you have to is absurd.)

- Have I planned the logistics of eating three square meals a day? (Trying to skimp on food is going to weaken you physically and will take its toll on your ability to do your best work.)

- Am I the sort of person who thinks well on my feet? In a festival environment, life is always going to throw you a curveball. Your show could fail to sell a single ticket, a thunderstorm could blast your sound system to smithereens during an outdoor show, your entire crew could get ringworm and decide to quit en masse—and if you're in charge, you're going to have to figure out how to proceed.

- Am I working with competent people? You're only as good as those who surround you. Although lots of performers do tour alone on the circuit, it's highly preferable to take an experienced stage manager (SM) with you, at minimum. Any additional crew or performance personnel beyond that must be professional, serious-minded, talented, and as committed to making the show work as you are. Waiting a few months or a year to hit the circuit can be the best move you ever make.

Fergus Linehan (the director of the Dublin Theatre Festival) warns, "Quite often, work shouldn't tour. It actually damages the company—it damages them financially, it damages their reputation, they're just not ready to go. They've had some sort of success somewhere, but actually, really good work doesn't necessarily translate and doesn't necessarily tour internationally. Even with the sort of festivals that pay good fees and pay all of the casts, you don't make any money, really. You have to put in a ferocious amount of work. It's always been interesting, different countries and why they travel there. Quebec is obviously a great example, where it's absolutely essential for those artists to travel because they need to keep that connection with Europe and in a way, it's how they define their own identity. So that's worth their while to go through all that trouble.

"Really ask yourself hard questions about why the hell you want to tour. Wanting to see the world is not a good enough reason. It's the companies that make a really long-term commitment to touring, and are constantly knocking on the door and trying to make it happen—they're the companies we as festival directors want to develop a relationship with; they are the ones we want to present more than once. But most of those companies have really established in their own minds why it's important for them."

If you do feel qualified and prepared, know that your audience will expect your very best—but when you give it, the rewards can be plentiful. "The audience on the fringe is very loyal," says Shannan Calcutt. "If you're going to go out this year and do your show and it's successful and people like you, they're coming back the next year and the next year. There are people on the fringe circuit who clear a good amount of money, and who live on it the rest of the year. I wouldn't say they're living high, but they're able to live as artists and spend the rest of the year creating their material and doing other shows. If you're going to tour the whole circuit, you're going to invest between eight and ten grand to do all the festivals, but then you've got at least sixty to eighty shows to bring that money back."

It's All About How You Apply Yourself

There is no more important element to the preliminary process of performing at any festival than the application procedure. Obviously, the major reason for this is brass-tacks practical: If you don't fill out and send in an application in a timely manner, you can't secure a performance slot.

This would appear to be common sense, but quite frankly, many playmakers on the fest scene are totally lax about taking care of the business of applications. Truth be told, many performers on the circuit are far more absorbed in the romance and creativity of their artistry than in making smart business moves—this isn't a criticism, but it is a fact. Festival offices have heard every excuse in the book for late or missing applications, and their personnel have been begged and sweet-talked and yelled at every which way but Sunday by performers whose lack of paperwork has jeopardized or nullified their chance to present. So right away, resolve to set yourself apart from the flaky flock and get your forms filled out accurately and early.

Early is a major buzzword here; for fringes that operate on a first-come, first-served basis, the faster you get your stuff submitted, the faster your berth will be confirmed. For selective festivals, sending your application materials in as soon as possible demonstrates that an organization is a priority for you, and shows respect. I've said it before, and I'll say it again: Always go to the a festival's Web site to check updated information before making contact. Make very careful note of application deadlines. On the fringe circuit, some fests are scheduled closely together so performers can move easily from one to another, so you may find yourself faced with a situation where you apply to one fest, but forget another's deadline is coming up right behind it, miss that second deadline, and have a gaping hole in your road schedule. Usually, you'll be able to download an application for a festival at its Web site. You'll fill it out, package it up with supplementary materials like your script, a performance video, resume, reviews, and the like, and mail it off with the required registration or application fees. In putting your packages together, resist the time-saving impulse to send the exact same cover letter out in duplicate—that's an amateur move. Instead, make mention in your correspondence what you like about the festival in terms of its mission and offerings. As long as you don't lay it on too thick, a genuine compliment that reflects your informed interest is always a nice touch.

Also, scout a fest carefully to make sure the work you're offering jibes with what they like to present. "I like solo work that is not necessarily the autobiographical therapy," Janet Munsil, producer of the Uno Festival, remarks. "'How I triumphed over adversity and learned to love myself' kinds of monologues. Really, those are all great personal stories, but we see so many every year. When we go through the applications, and we see dozen of applications, so many are people telling their personal stories without, necessarily, the theatrical element we want to present. So we want to show people that solo shows aren't what they think they are. We try to do a broader range of solo shows, like dance and clown. We had one musical; we had performance art; we incorporated visual art. We try to show as broad a spectrum as we can. It's really about the talent of the performer. I think that's why it's so important to have a videotape, in this case—because it's not just about your wonderful script. It's also about how do you grab an audience and make them pay attention to you for forty-five minutes or whatever? You have to have incredible force as a performer. The shows in the festival can be quite electrifying sometimes, when somebody can pull off the technical feat of being the one person onstage. It's very intimidating.

"My husband, Paul Terry, does a solo show called *The Ugly Duchess*. We've been taking it to one fringe a year because we feel too old to do the circuit! My husband says it's like getting on a train. You think you're never going to be able to do it, and you get onstage and start, and suddenly it's over. You've just got to go along with it."

If you've got an intelligent question or two for a festival office before sending off your application, don't hesitate to ask—but be respectful of the office's often-limited time. Try e-mailing your query before calling. Any good fest will be glad to reply if you keep your question clear and short. Some festivals are generous enough to spend as much time as they can answering play-makers' concerns. "Working in the Fringe office is an odd experi-ence," says Paul Gudgin. "There are a lot of periods of the year where it's just almost like working in any office environment, because parts of the year we're quite removed from the whole business of the arts and performing. But the one thing that I think all of us enjoy, and the one thing that's very special about working here, is that we spend a lot of our time talking to performers wanting advice. They want advice and support and help in how they can bring a show to the Fringe, and how they can make it work best for them. I think the thing that is most gratifying for us at the Fringe is, when you meet someone in the autumn, or at any point in the year, and you advise them about how they might bring a show to the Fringe, and how they might do that best, and all these sorts of issues, and then when you see that come to fruition—a show you spoke to somebody about in December is suddenly appearing and selling and work-ing very well on the Fringe in the following August. From my own point of view, I'm sure that's what gives me, and many other members of this team, satisfaction—seeing performers and performances you've helped benefit from that."

Knowing a bit about how your work is going to be evaluated once it's submitted can be very helpful; try to read up on the Web about this as much as possible (rather than ask a fest office about it directly, because that will make you look a tad desperate). At Humana, a panel of senior staff members takes a very hands-on approach to play selection, as Zan Sawyer-Dailey describes: "Those people are reading the plays all year long. At a certain point during the summer, they begin to narrow the list down—they'll start with about fifty, and then will drop ten and then will narrow it down to thirty. At that point, the artistic director, Mark Masterson, and I begin to read these plays as well. There's about eight of us who really get into the thick of it starting the first of the summer, so that by the end of the summer, we've usually identified ten, maybe fifteen plays that we feel it would help us to hear them aloud. So we usually go to the playwrights at that point and say, 'This is not a test. We're just trying to learn a little bit more—do you care if we come into New York, and you can work with us, and we'll have a reading of your play?'

So we sort of do a little play reading series in New York some-time in late August, and we'll hear about five to ten plays in about five days. And the playwrights help us—they sort of tell us who are good actors that they like. We don't rehearse them—the actors come in, sit down at the table, and give it their best shot. The playwright may give them a few tips ahead of time. It's really a lot of fun. We meet a lot of interesting people this way, people who may not necessarily be able to come to Louisville for the project, but who support it. It gives the playwrights great oppor-tunity to be involved in that process and to hear their play. And then we kind of talk to them and sort of say, 'What do you think? Where do you think the play is going? Do you think there's any way we could be of assistance to you?' Because sometimes if we see some things that we think need to be fixed and the playwright isn't interested in those, they're not wrong, but we may not necessarily have a mutual viewpoint on this, so we may not be able to assist the play."

If it turns out a festival decides to pass on your work, don't get angry; be gracious. It's okay to ask for feedback on why the decision was made, and for suggestions on a few changes you could conceivably make. Ask politely if the festival would look at your piece again in the future, if you do decide to make changes it suggests. It's very possible you'll get a second shot, especially if you leave a positive impression in mind.

Scouting A Festival in Person

The Web and phone can tell you a lot, but a really ideal way to get a feel for a particular festival is to visit it in person, especially if you've found out you have won a spot to work at it. That way, you can conceivably see some shows, talk to participating artists, and spend face time with a fest producer or two. In general, this practice is encouraged by all types of fests—the more familiar you are with an organization up close, the better work you can do for and with it.

Leah Cooper, executive director of the Minnesota Fringe, is living proof that immersing yourself into the scene full-on truly pays off. "I moved to Minnesota seven years ago from southern California," she recalls. "I've always been a theater junkie, with a particular passion for work that is original, raw, funky, and not overburdened by glitzy, expensive production elements. I discovered the Fringe Festival here during my second summer, and was immediately hooked. For the next couple of years I was an avid attendee, catching forty or more shows at the Fringe each summer.

"During this time, I was focused on practicalities of relocation, but eventually I wanted to return to my lifelong avocation of directing, writing, producing, and performing theater. The Fringe, with its wide spectrum of companies, venues, and performers, was an amazing opportunity to quickly acquaint myself with the entire theater scene here.

"In 1999, I signed up to produce my own show in the Fringe. This gave me a chance to meet the people running the organization—a surprisingly small and unpaid group. The executive director at the time, Dean J. Seal, and I hit it off immediately and had many exciting conversations about shared vision and hope for what the Fringe did and could grow to be here.

"Soon I found myself on the board of directors, then (became) the board president, then a volunteer managing director. Meanwhile, I had a busy career as an independently consulting software engineer. After the 2001 festival, Dean was exhausted from four years of stewarding the festival through its most rapid period of growth (425 percent increase in attendance in four years). He resigned from the board and asked me to take over. It was good timing because I was bored with software, and tired of splitting my attention between such different endeavors. Much to the shock of my family and friends, I said yes to five times the work for one-fifth the salary—and so, with no regrets, here I am."

Cooper's story proves that you never know how far initial contact with a fest can take you. In planning that first encounter, call in advance and ask to make an appointment to talk with someone in the festival office. Introducing yourself at the outset can help you down the line in terms of making helpful contacts. A planned meeting is also a time-economical way to ask questions (for both you and a festival staff member).

In terms of who to talk to, of course the artistic director is ideal, but he or she is often unavailable. A lower-level producer or literary manager, although quite busy as well, can probably make time to see you and will most likely be able to address questions you may have, or hook you up with others who can help. No matter who you speak with, a face-to-face meeting is bound to give you a sense for how it feels to work at the festival—both through experience and anecdote. "One of the things we throw at people is, we don't have a lot of money, but we do have time and skills," says Ko Fest's artistic director, Sabrina Hamilton. "In most festival situations, people are getting into the theater the day of, the day before. We really have people get in Monday, and they don't open till Friday, and the theater's all theirs. So we've also become a place where, people who've made a piece and sometimes have toured it, but haven't had chance to rework it—you've got a piece and you know it's not quite right, you know this section needs work—we can provide the time, the skills.

"It comes from years of touring in festival situations where you're really frustrated! We've started to address those kinds of things. One of the things that's unusual is we really tell the interns that we don't have a house way of working. We work the way the artist works. One week we may laugh it up, being asked for our opinions, having a very raucous atmosphere, and the next week it may be Zen-garden invisible. What we try to start with at Ko is, What's the fantasy? What is the best way that the art can happen?"

You can also ask questions about the audience's demographic while observing it, if you visit while a fest is actually up. Jenny Magnus, co-founder of the Rhinoceros Theater Festival, gives a good example. "Our demographic is all over the place, depending upon the artists whose work is showing," says Magnus. "I have often written into grant proposals that Curious (the Curious Theater Branch, this festival's parent organization), and by extension, Rhino, serve a particular community. Not a demographic community, or one described by gender, or economics, but we serve the community of the intelligentsia in Chicago. A lot of artists come to Rhino, but also people who love theater and are not artists, and also young people interested in youth culture will come looking for the next cool thing. As for producers coming, I wouldn't know one if he bit me, so I don't know if they are coming or not."

Here are some other smart questions to ask in a face-to-face meeting:

- How do critics fit into the festival scene?
- How do audience members express feedback? Are there symposiums or talkback sessions organized for the playmakers post-performance?
- Can I see a sample venue space and maybe speak to a technician today?
- How much tech time am I guaranteed in space before my show goes up?
- Do you require artists and companies to carry any specific insurance to work here?
- Are participants ever fined or penalized for "infractions" like missing festival meetings or taking too long to set up or strike a show?
- Does the festival take any long-term financial interest or option in my work if it gets commercial pick-up, or gets published?
- Plus, ask every question you can think of regarding specific artistic, production, financial, or scheduling arrangements.

If you don't like the answer to any question you receive, probe further. If you still don't like what you hear, DON'T SIGN ANYTHING. (More about smart business practices in chapter 5.) There are lots of fish in the festival sea, and you may just have to cast your line out again.

The Artists' Angle

If you've seen a show at a particular fest and really admire an artist's performance or writing, don't be shy; wait around after the show and introduce yourself to this person. Give your rave review, then ask for a couple of minutes of this person's time to inquire about how working at this particular fest actually feels. (Offering to buy a couple of artists dinner is usually a very welcome invitation, and gives you the chance to shoot the breeze for a good chunk of time.)

Some of the points you may want to inquire about:

• If an audition or tryout performance is required of a participant before final acceptance, find out what exactly it entails.
• Ask about relations between competing artists. Is the vibe supportive? Ugly? Distant?
• How's the quality of life in terms of backstage space, tech and prop availability, and rehearsal time? Does the festival staff show artists kindness, respect, and support?
• Are playwrights pressured to change their work as the fest sees fit, even if they feel uncomfortable about it?
• How quickly does the festival pay artists?
• Is dealing with the audience a treat or a nightmare? Are the crowds respectful and interested, or noisy and obnoxious? Does organized feedback (if applicable) work well?
• Is it easy to get reviewed or written up in the local press?
• Is it just plain old-fashioned fun here? (If not, the festival had better be peerlessly prestigious, or the financial benefits should be mind-boggling.)

Most of the Time, Things Work Out

Take heart: The majority of a playmaker's festival experiences turn out to be just fine. Most major fests (certainly the ones highlighted in this book) work hard to make their gatherings as artist- and audience-friendly as possible. Okay, a trip to a fringe isn't going to compare to a weekend at the Ritz, but you know that going in. Keep your expectations realistic, and beautiful creative things can happen. Here's a memorable example:

"*The Car* was a particularly novel concept of site-specific work in the [Minnesota] Fringe four years ago," says Leah Cooper. "Produced by Skewed Visions [a Minneapolis-based performance troupe], it put the audience in the back seat of three different cars. The show took place in the front seat while the cars drove around downtown Minneapolis. Each car was a different story, very driven (pardon the pun) by the experience of being in a car. Audiences loved this show! Now Skewed Visions does site-specific work all year long, and there is a growing culture of site-specific work here with more artists and audiences trying it every year."

4

Before You Hit the Road

So you've applied to a few festivals, and you've been accepted at one or two you really want to do. You've visited the places you'll be working at in person, talked to personnel and artists till you feel confident you know the score, drawn up a budget, packed your car, and grabbed your SM. Nothing left to do but hit the highway, right?

Wrong. Unpack the car.

If you haven't learned anything about real, concrete planning in your life, this chapter's here to teach you. We now break down the festival planning process as it pertains to sharpening your material so you can show it off to best advantage; quality-of-life issues; and points of practicality.

Material Concerns

In order for your show to survive and thrive on a competitive festival level, you have to take complete inventory of where it stands quality-wise, no matter how often you've performed it and how well you think you know what you're doing. It's tough to see your work objectively the longer you've been living with it; you almost grow numb to its impact, be that impact good or bad.

Your first step in preparing work for the road is to have a totally objective artist take a look at it—someone whose opinion you respect, but who hasn't seen it a million times (preferably someone who hasn't seen it at all). If you have a mentor, maybe a teacher or director you've worked well with in the past, ask him/her to evaluate where your material's at, either by reading your best draft (if you're a playwright) or watching a run-through. This person can give you notes with a fresh perspective, and with a professional take on advice that will make your show the best it can be. Shannan Calcutt's college mentor not only helped her with the creation of her successful character, but continues to provide her with clarity and guidance—as do her audiences.

"I studied at the University of Victoria in British Columbia," says Calcutt. "In the fourth year, we did a lot of character mask and improv and commedia dell'arte, and so I wanted to work more physically like this, more creative, where you can create your own material. So I went to the Dell'Arte International School of Physical Theatre—it's a professional actor training program. The whole idea there is to encourage actors who want to create their own material. Every Friday, you're presenting your own material—it may be only five minutes long, but it's something you've created that week.

At Dell'Arte, I met Sue Morrison, who is a clown teacher based in Toronto. Sue was teaching a clown workshop in Canada, so I got lucky and took it. It was in that workshop that I started to really find my clown. I talked to Sue about making a show together, and that became the first Izzy show, *Burnt Tongue*. It toured the fringe circuit in 1999. It was really successful; I made a second show, then had an idea for a trilogy. We actually created three shows together, which I've toured three years in a row on the fringe circuit.

"In clown, you don't really have a show without an audience. When I was building the show, I was making it with Sue, and I would just basically play for her on my feet, improvising. She would videotape the action, and I'd make my script from there. I opened my first show in Ottawa at the Fringe there in 1999, and it was very scary! But in clown, the audience is your partner, and it was amazing. I got great laughs, got laughs in places I never anticipated—and of course, didn't get them in places I'd planned for! The first ten shows I do of a new show, I'm always changing things based on the audience response, and trying new things out, trying maybe a totally different ending, a new entrance, cutting material. The Fringe has been an amazing place to do that. It's an affordable place to create new material, and it's definitely an extremely successful place for testing the waters."

Once you've gotten a little outside perspective on your project, make a list of the things you agree need fixing. Here's a quick-scan guide to the most common areas you'll probably want to spruce up:

Rewrites

Check your text for weak or unclear plotlines, holes, bad or confusing character development, clunky dialogue, outrageous plot twists, and anything that makes you cringe. A nice pace that keeps the plot moving along is essential to win favor at any playwrights' forum—but surprisingly, an unconventional structure is often applauded. Thomas Morrissey, artistic director of the Genesius Guild, makes it his business to study past innovation. "We've looked at historically some of the most outstanding theatrical pieces. Those that have made a major impact have not copied or come from things that necessarily came immediately before, and some of them were quite commercially successful and yet they took risks that would make one think that maybe they weren't going to be viable. Take *A Chorus Line*, for example—it was a show that was incredibly impactful, and kind of changed the way people looked at theater at that point. Even if you go back to like, *Oklahoma*—*Oklahoma*, when it opened, was considered bad structural form. There were no musicals that were structured that way, investors actually tried to pull their money out of the show, and the cast was kind of betting on how long the show would last—I think the highest guess was three days. And yet now, that show is considered classic form."

Mark Scharf has built a solid reputation as a lauded playwright. His work has been produced in New York, Washington, Los Angeles, and London, to name just a few cities. Now chairman of the Baltimore Playwright's Festival, his initial experience with that fest was a writer. He describes his developmental experience at the BPF, plus shares some thoughts on quality development as a whole.

"I worked with a director once; the first thing he said to me was, 'I prefer to work with dead playwrights or playwrights who live out of state.' Obviously, I knew we were in trouble here. With the Baltimore Playwright's Festival, though, the import is, Here's an opportunity to improve the text, as opposed to, This is a brilliant, finished piece of work I'm never going to touch again. When I'm finished with a play at this festival, I feel like I've got a handle on it. It's in much better shape to submit to people.

"I learned about the festival through the Dramatists Guild in New York. I sent in a script of mine cold, and I got a phone call from Rodney S. Bonds, the chairman at the time. He was also running a small theater company called the Harbor Theater Company, and he invited me to see their production of *The Miracle Worker*. They gave me a tour of the space and I met everybody. They did a play of mine in '94. It was nice. I felt at home, and I kept submitting, and they kept producing them within the different theater companies that are involved. The BPF I've always likened more to a confederacy. There's not an artistic director or committee that oversees a theme. The individual theaters retain their prerogative to produce the plays they want to produce.

"Most playwrights I know here really listen to the response to their plays, and do rewrites. When you're sitting on the stage after a reading and listening to an audience discussion, for example, you don't have to say a word. You don't have to defend yourself—you're not on trial. You can just sit and listen. If you want to talk, that's fine, but you don't have to. You can just smile and say, 'Thank you.' There is always somebody who thinks that what they've written is gospel and golden. But most playwrights I know will take something and rewrite it. Even if they initially resist it, you can't argue with the fact that an audience is slumped in their chairs, or rattling their programs. Those are the things you look for: When were they leaning forward? When were they sitting back? You have to pay attention to those details.

"I've learned the rules of dealing with a cast, especially in terms of working on a new play. I talk to the director, and the director talks to the actors. If I do talk to them directly, I've clued the director in beforehand, because there can only be one captain of the ship. Actors—God bless them, it's human nature—everybody has an agenda. Maybe they'll come to you and say, 'Don't you think my character would do this and that?' And you say, 'Well, yeah, they might,' and they go to the director and say, 'Well, the PLAYWRIGHT said . . .' So you don't want to get into that kind of a problem.

"You have to learn how to filter. There's always going to be the person who wants to show off how much he knows. Everybody wants to rewrite your play, so you have to filter that and get down to, Okay, what is the *problem* that they're addressing, as opposed to what is the solution that they are offering?"

Directorial Logistics

If you're a playwright, and you're going to be taking your director along to a festival that expects a lot—this may sound brutal, but—make sure he or she can deliver. "Most often, I would say at least 85 percent of the time, playwrights do bring directors with them," says Zan Sawyer-Dailey (artistic manager at the Actors' Theatre of Louisville) regarding the Humana Festival of New Plays. "While the playwright does not have complete control of that process—we maintain control of that process—it is certainly in our interest to find the director that the playwright is most comfortable with.

"What we look at in that process is, Where has that person directed in the past? Interestingly enough, what interests us most is their regional theater credits. It's a very different mindset to be directing in a large regional institution than to be directing for the commercial theater or the Broadway theater. That's very important to us because when a director is going to be one of seven, it's essential that they understand the entire operation of practice. They need to be able to work inside the institution, not against the institution. It is our experience that many, many freelance directors who come to work at our theater for the first time bring with them a kind of built-in defense mechanism, which we very carefully disassemble.

"We spend a great deal of time upfront to sort of disarm them and allow them to trust us and allow them to know we really will take care of them—not just get them through it, but really help them, give them the production that they want, with limited resources. For instance, we have in our institution, across the boards, an open rehearsal policy. Anybody inside the family can go see any rehearsal at any time, unless it's specifically announced ahead of time, for reasons having to do with the nature of the work, that that rehearsal will be closed. That's hard for some directors. It's hard for some directors to understand that our technical staff has to see run-throughs at certain points, because they don't have any more time to come back. They're gonna go into tech for three other shows, so they won't get back into that rehearsal. So we structure the rehearsal schedule, and tell them when they have to have the run-throughs, and when they have to be up on their feet. We have very specific deadlines about when props can be changed, and those kinds of elements, because we're taking care of our resident staff as well.

"Aside from those kinds of logistics, the other things that we are interested in with directors are: people who are willing to actually make decisions quickly and live with them; people who enjoy the practice of working with a large number of artists, so that they may get involved with our apprentice company, they may get involved with assistant directors who are students. We want them to be able to hang out in our bar and talk to our patrons. So there is a social aspect to the organization as well that's very important to us."

Brush-Up Rehearsals

When you're building a show to take on tour, you can't get enough rehearsal. As you get closer and closer to completing a piece, analyze your run-throughs for trouble spots: awkward staging, lags or gaps in scene pacing, forgotten or dropped character motivation, dropped lines, and sloppy, slow, or mistake-riddled tech cues.

Start brush-up rehearsals no later than a month prior to leaving for your first festival. A three-to-five-day-a-week schedule is not too demanding—you want the show to run like clockwork by the time you leave town. Also, keep in mind that the more rehearsal you get now, the more limber you'll remain later, when finding time and space to rehearse while traveling can be nearly impossible.

Test Performances

Use your own company's house, borrow a house, or pay for a couple of performances somewhere—just have test performances! You won't regret running changes and adjustments before a live crowd. Invite friends and fans, sure, but also lure perfect strangers in however you can. Slot at least three test runs, and write up a brief audience questionnaire to hand out. After the show, ask audience members to write down their responses to queries like: Was the play easy to understand? What did you like least about it? What character was your favorite and why? Was the sound clear? Did the play feel like it moved to fast? Too slow? At just the right pace?

In addition to feedback forms, hold your own symposium after each performance and let the audience discuss the play's pluses and minuses. Don't be sensitive if somebody slams you! You've got to get used to your flaws being pointed out by patrons—they will almost certainly be at festival. Running your own talkback session gives you a sense of control (however delusional that really may be) over the proceedings, and that makes the medicine go down a little easier at first.

A related point: If you can start off your festival experience at a small-scale fest, do so. It helps ease you in to the whole festival process, and you can also practice talking to audience members on a more manageable level—which you most certainly have to do in order to get them to see your show. "I wanted to have a run of my show before I got to a bigger city, before I knew I'd be competing with a lot more shows, so I could arrive there with some confidence," says Calcutt. "When I first started out, I had no idea. I had postcards made for the show to hand out—I didn't even have posters, because it wasn't in my budget. I was going to cities I'd never been to, and I had no idea what to expect.

"I was surprised, actually, how amazing the Fringe was. Really, the press is so supportive—some cities a lot more than others. In Winnipeg, I had so many noon shows, and people were coming! There are hard-core fringers who want to come out and see the show, and you get reviewed.

"It's hard not to do well, I would think, on the Fringe, because your audience is there—it's just getting them into your show and letting them know about it. I was handing out postcards and chatting up the show—that is something you get better at. That's a whole other skill as an artist. When I didn't want to talk about the show, I'd just get in my clown and take my clown out there chatting, trying to get people to come see her, and that was easier. Sometimes, when I didn't want to call the press—I'd think, oh, I'm calling too much, or they're not interested, and I'd get a bit down—I'd just have my clown call and leave messages. I think that's more fun for the press as well. Find creative things—it's a producer's job to sell your show and you're an artist, so how do you make it fun? How do you make it creative?" (See the end of chapter 5 for more specific information on marketing yourself at a festival.)

Design for Living

Once your material's up to snuff, it's time to focus on logistics. Yep, our favorite things to think about—running out of money, getting stranded, getting sick, and wanting to strangle the annoying travel companion in the van seat next to you. But if we think about these potential pitfalls now, we can actually stop them from happening, so this phase of planning can actually be kind of fun.

Let's talk through these essentials one at a time.

The Beauty of Scheduling

Before you do anything else, grab your festival folder file box right now. As you've received acceptances/confirmations from various fests, no doubt you've been neatly organizing them in the proper place . . . oh, you haven't been? Then dive under your bed right now, and yank out that paperwork.

Now, using a blank calendar, write in the dates you'll be leaving to journey to each fest (give yourself generous advance arrival time), plus the actual fest rehearsal and performance dates. Make sure no fests overlap or overrun each other!

Another thing, while we're on the subject of scheduling: Have you stayed on schedule in regard to responding to those fests you intend to accept a performance slot at? If not, do so immediately.

Different types of festivals slot their performance times in different ways. For instance, huge fringes with hundreds of shows to schedule often resort to the democratic system of first-come, first-served (especially if they're unjuried). In other words, the first company to get the old application and fees in gets the first available performance slot on the first day the fest will be up.

Juried fringes tend to be a bit more methodical. This type of fest's powers-that-be are more likely to slot an established, invited performer (a Sarah Jones, say) on a Saturday night at 8:00 P.M., as opposed to a Thursday afternoon at 3:15. This type of slotting is good for box office, plain and simple.

Respected venues like the Humana Festival will probably simply assign dates, which you are, in most cases, expected to accept.

Speaking of weekends at 8:00 P.M., as opposed to the middle of workday afternoons, bear in mind that the hundreds of shows that are part of a festival might only take place in a very few venues, which means that your 12:00 P.M. show in that little black box might be preceded by a show at 9:30 A.M. and followed by one at 2:30 P.M. That means that three different casts and crews are running around during the hiatuses between shows, either setting up or tearing down, putting on costumes or taking them off. It's all got to work like clockwork, so that by the time the beleaguered house staff has the third audience in its seats, the curtain is ready to rise on show number three.

So, really, you don't have a whole lot of control over when you're scheduled, right? Well, if it's really important to you for logical reasons that your show take place at a certain time (it takes place outdoors at sunset, and the natural light is part of your artistic statement), then you can certainly try to negotiate. See if you can work out a switch with another company that's unhappy with its designated slot, if at all possible, then get the change approved pronto (well in advance of the festival run). This is imperative because the fest you're at is creating press materials that announce whole performances that are taking place. Therefore, you can't just switch things around. Another obvious reason to discuss such a change well in advance is that most likely, you won't know what other groups are performing, let alone which ones (if any) are unhappy with their venues. Always talk to fest personnel as soon as possible about such matters. Personnel can be quite helpful and flexible. (For instance, a fest like the Minnesota Fringe is known for its consistent efforts to accommodate site-specific work all over the city of Minneapolis.)

So what can you do if your assigned venue is technically inadequate, or dangerous, or stifling hot? You can speak up, if the space is a hazard to performers or audience members. If your concerns are more cosmetic (the curtain has a huge hole in the middle, or the dressing room is the size of a glove compartment), don't be a diva. At many festivals you'll have to be a good sport, and rise above the inevitable inconvenience or two. If your shows good enough, the audience won't care where it's sitting to watch it.

Mapping Things Out

Veteran fest performers, especially on Canada's fringe circuit, travel east to west, as that's the order that the festivals play out in. Even if you're traveling to just a fest or two, you still have to put the same amount of effort into map work. Plot out your driving route, estimating mileage and gas needs, and try to pin down motels along the way, if that's how you intend to sleep. Use the Web to learn about good, cheap restaurants along your route as well.

Networking will quickly help you out. "On the fringe circuit, when I began, I knew no one on the circuit and I did it on my own," says Shannan Calcutt. "You just meet people on the circuit, and you find your family. When you tour more than once, so do the same people. It's very easy—I flew to Ottawa, but then I had my car in Winnipeg, so I toured from there on and shared the gas with other performers in my vehicle. What happens a lot is that people will rent a van together and end up sharing travel expenses that way."

Budgeting

As we covered in chapter 3, the financial planning system of three times the amount of cash you need per month is the safest way to go. To reiterate: Sit down and plot out all of your basic expenses for thirty-one days. Include lodging, meals, gas, technical expenses, and a $10 emergency per diem per day for every person in your group, plus anything else you know you'll need to spend. Triple that total; this is your fail-safe budget for a one-month trip.

Now look at your cash reserves. Do you have triple the monthly total available to you? If not, consider taking out a loan, or borrowing the cash from a family member or friend (especially if this is your first trip out, and you don't have lay of the land yet). Put the excess money into traveler's checks or a secure pre-paid travel credit card (American Express offers a good one) and then DON'T SPEND IT UNLESS YOU HAVE AN EMERGENCY. Repay any outstanding balances to your loved ones as soon as you return.

You also should budget in at least $600 for promotional materials (like photos, postage, postcards, and press kits—more specifics on these in chapter 5), which should be prepared prior to your trip.

Unions

A large majority of fringe performers are non-union. However, some union performers do work on the fringe scene and are plentiful at many other festivals. Often, a playwrights' festival will incorporate members of its own company into a new works production, and as that festival is under the auspices of a theater affiliated with Actors Equity Association (in the United States), you have no union issues to deal with. Traveling on your own with union actors, especially to other countries, is potentially a highly restrictive, difficult enterprise, however—you need to put up a bond, set up a payroll system, and arrange insurance, at the minimum. It's imperative you make arrangements with Equity. Contact the union as soon as possible to do so.

Insurance

What exactly do you need? Definitely health and travel insurance for yourself; maybe accidental death or injury, too. As for your company members, call fests you'll be working at in advance and ask which automatically cover participants; you may need to provide supplemental coverage in some (rare) cases. You may also need workers' comp (you definitely will need to make such arrangements with Actors Equity if you're using union members). Ask any union you make arrangements with what their insurance requirements are if they are not clearly spelled out to you. (Chances are such insurance guidelines will be, and you'll have to sign paperwork assuming responsibility for it.)

Overseas Travel

You need a passport for sure; shots, and a work visa, if applicable. Work with your festival to find out exactly how it assists foreign playmakers in coming overseas—they will have up-to-date info, or will be able to direct you toward the appropriate resources.

Lodging

Don't leave sleeping arrangements to chance. Before making expensive hotel or motel reservations, check with your fests for their latest accommodation guidelines (which can change frequently). Also, if you're a Canadian artist, many fringes will billet you—that is, arrange for and cover the costs of your rooms on the road.

The fringe circuit is also well known for hooking up visiting artists with hosting fringe fans. This has its pluses and minuses. "You're staying in people's houses, and you probably wouldn't be able to afford it otherwise," says TJ Dawe. "I'm eternally grateful that people want to do that. Sometimes, it's a guest room, and sometimes it's the couch, and sometimes it's the floor. Quite often, you can make friends with people who have a good place, and they'll invite you back the next year. That's happened with me in a few cities.

"Sometimes it's not so great. Sometimes people kind of think of you as their pet. They're really excited to have you staying with them, and they want to cook for you and show you around town. Quite often, you really just want to be left alone.

"There's a horror story that I'm actually writing into my new show. On my first fringe tour in 1998, I came down with mono partway through the tour. I was in Saskatoon and a heat wave hit, and the place where I was staying—it was a single mother with two kids, and the kids were with the father for these particular two weeks. I have never, ever in my life been in such a messy house! It was disgusting! I don't have the highest standards, but this was unbelievable! The litter box had never been cleaned, the dishes were stacked almost to the ceiling, the carpet had never been vacuumed, the bathroom had never been cleaned. The mattress that I was on, it was like a little kids' bed, it was covered in piss and shit stains. And I had mono! And I couldn't swallow—it was mono mimicking tonsillitis! It was a hellish point. And at that point, I was still intending to do my show, although I ended up canceling. That's probably the worst place I've ever stayed."

You may think sleeping in your car or van might be a better bet at times, but it can be extraordinarily dangerous to do so (especially in an area you don't know). Definitely talk to office staff at your fest about the best options they've got available instead, and try to make the best of it wherever you happen to land—it won't be forever.

Food

Again, budgeting is paramount. If you think it will be more appetizing to plop yourself down at a greasy spoon rather than exist on peanut butter sandwiches made on the shoulder of an expressway, figure in the cost of at least one big restaurant meal per day. Then you can eat nutritious but inexpensive breakfast food (like yogurt or granola bars, for instance, which are available at nearly any convenience store) and a light lunch (like a take-out salad). This way you'll get your vitamins without breaking the bank.

Interpersonal Stresses

Is the way your SM obsessively flosses between every tooth in her mouth in the rearview mirror at least three times a day starting to drive you nuts? If so, put down that plastic butter knife, pull over the van, and get some air for a couple of minutes.

On the road, even the best working relationships can head south. "If you go out in a group and things start going weird or wrong, you start blaming other people," remarks Charlie Ross. "You start looking for problems within the company, and they can drive you apart—except you're stuck. You're doing the show, you're stuck in a van together, you're seeing each other every day, and it's terrible. Plus, you're financially tied together. Your first time out can be terribly traumatic—you need to be friends in a way that almost goes beyond friendship."

There's no way everybody in your group can avoid getting on each other's nerves at some point, so know this in advance. Figure in a little time apart every day, even for a half-hour or so. Bring a set of noise-blocking headphones or a Walkman along as well to instantly drop out of an annoying situation. But, as Charlie points out, while this enforced closeness "can be a humongous stress upon a friendship, if things are going well, then it feels really great."

Packing List
Here are some suggestions.

- Two sets of copies of all the paperwork you'll need at every fest you'll attend (leave the originals at home). Include two copies of every registration fee check you've written as well. Also, two sets of all union paperwork, plus your festival file box containing two copies of each relevant piece of info you've collected about each fest you'll be working at.
- Duplicate sets of your keys.
- Plastic utensils, Styrofoam or plastic cups, and paper plates.
- Your pillow from home.
- Lots of spare underwear (laundry is a rare priority on the fest circuit).
- Clothes you can use in lots of different combos (jeans, black and white T-shirts, flat shoes, boots, or sandals).
- A Swiss army knife.
- A trusty watch.
- A bike. (Absolutely invaluable, according to many festivals insiders—transit options can be spotty in many cities, and venues often lie far apart. Make a habit out of locking it up so it doesn't get stolen).

• Two copies of your Filofax or datebook, or two PDAs containing all personal and business contact information (in case you lose one).

• A pre-paid cell phone or phone card. You can use it to call home on a limited basis or in an emergency, and you won't get tangled up in long-distance or cell phone plan bills.

• Your favorite music, and a Walkman to play it on.

Pack everything in a large but lightweight duffle bag or knapsack. Try to limit yourself to two bags, max; you'll be glad you did.

Any last thoughts on what to take? "You really learn quickly what you can live without," says Charlie Ross. "You can take your camera. You can take a couple of books, but don't take too many books, because the coolest thing about getting to new cities is that they all have used bookstores. I tend to bring a nice set of clothes even if I don't get a chance to use them. Every time I've been out, I've had a suit. Take a tie, if you're a guy; you might find yourself on television, and you don't want to look like a scumbag.

"Take something to write down notes, but I would not take my favorite diary with me. You need to ask yourself, If my bag gets stolen, what can't I live without? Don't take your favorite clothes. If you can afford it, buy yourself a new pair of shorts, pants, a couple new shirts, whatever. You don't have to go crazy buying Armani stuff, but buy something new, because if you're taking something old and tired with you already, it's gonna be beyond old and tired before you're done. It's like having a new set of armor. You feel that as you gain experience, that experience is also being absorbed into these clothes. They become endowed with something bigger. These shorts become battle shorts, absolutely!

"Take a little bit of money—it can be just a hundred bucks, even—in case you want to have a hotel room, because damn it, you bloody well deserve it. If you want to have a shower for as long as you want, if you want to have your own space and watch

TV and not give a shit about anybody, that hundred dollars can feel like the biggest luxury in the world. If you don't end up using it, great, then you obviously don't need it. But you can save it up for the right time, and it's a reward, and it's the kind of gift that only you can give to yourself."

Spending the Money You Make

In a word: don't.

Save all of the money you can, outside of doling out cuts and/or payroll, till you come off the road. You need a clear head and a little time off in order to figure out what to do with your profit: Save it? Put it right back into another trip? What we cover next will help you get a solid grasp on these and other financial basics.

5

The Complete Festival Business Primer

Marketing, contracts, commitments, legal issues—this isn't the kind of stuff an artist like you has to worry about, right? Wrong. You own two valuable commodities—your talent and your material—and a lot of people don't possess such riches. So if they're unscrupulous, they're going to want to steal, or at least take heavy advantage of, what you've got.

That's not to say that the fest scene is infested with vultures in producers' clothing trying to swindle every talented young whippersnapper they meet. It is to say, be smart and self-protective. Look out for the best interests of yourself, and your show, before anything else; nobody else is going to watch out for you.

Let's go over the major business issues you have to be mindful of.

Signing on the Dotted Line

First rule of the big business thumb: *Never sign a contract without talking to a lawyer.* You need a good attorney—preferably one with an entertainment background/practice—to read over every line of any contract you're presented with, from the most innocuous-looking performance agreement to the most complicated publishing deal.

What's okay in regard to standard terms for a festival appearance? In general, the contract you're presented with should contain the following points:

- Performance dates should be clearly noted.
- All technical requirements to be carried out by both sides should be noted.
- All financial profit splits and payouts should be noted, preferably with payout dates clearly stipulated.
- Any future stake an entity may wish to exercise in regard to royalties, publications, future productions, or options should be noted and clearly distinguished by negotiated and agreed-upon percentages and length/period of agreement dates.
- Every point should be negotiable, and the contract should not be considered executed unless both parties have signed the contract.

Your attorney can give you even more detailed, nuanced info, and can do the tough-talking for you. Don't be afraid to ask him/her even the most elementary questions, and don't be afraid of walking away from a deal if you don't like the consequences.

Not to make you paranoid, but it also pays to be extra careful when negotiating because of a recent trend in the fest world: financial collapse. In early 2004, the festival world was rocked by the sudden announcement that the famed Seattle Fringe Festival was declaring bankruptcy. The Fringe had written an open letter to the theater community in Washington State on its official Web site in late 2003, warning that it was in big money trouble; many artists were understandably concerned at that time. After the bankruptcy announcement, it was reported that many Fringe artists were still owed their profits from the previous year.

Rumors started flying during the winter of 2004 as to which fringe might be the next to go under. As of press time, no additional festivals have folded (although even well-respected fests like the New York International Fringe have made no secret of the fact that funds are tight). Considering the financial climate, it's very important to get the specifics of your money deal agreed to in writing from the word go. Ask your lawyer to help you structure contract wording so it benefits you most in case of any form of unforeseen festival financial issue.

The Wonderful World of Funding

Can you actually get money to finance your touring on the festival circuit? Conceivably, sure. You need to bring a strong resume, a track record proving your success, experience on the road, and good reviews to the table, though. If you hope to receive nonprofit funding, either you have to have nonprofit status yourself, or else you have to be working under the sponsorship of a nonprofit umbrella organization that can accept funding for you (like The Field, in New York City, *www.thefield.org*).

For up-to-date resource info on how and where to apply for grants, a great font of information is the Foundation Center in New York City. This fabulous and artist-friendly organization can help you answer any funding question, and walk you through proposal researching and writing from soup to nuts. (See the appendixes for more artist resource listings).

So what other options do you have? You are probably going to have to get creative. I've heard of a beloved bartender whose customers gave him the money to take his show to Edinburgh. I've also heard of a high school drama club in Massachusetts that sold raffle tickets to win a car—and yes, they, too, made it to Edinburgh. There's always your friends and family . . . they are probably good for some "sponsorship" and they can also help you brainstorm and trumpet your goals to the community at large. After all, people love to be part of a good success story.

Making Ends Meet

The key to thriving and surviving artistically on the road lies in foolproof planning, and that includes financial forethought. Let's get real here: It's impossible to focus on doing the best work you can if you're freaking out internally over how you're going to afford your next meal, let alone the gas to get home. Making a living wage at a festival (or even drawing a salary while touring the entire scene) requires thinking ahead in regard to procedure and production concerns.

Charlie Ross got a crash course in financial management the first time he toured in a group situation. "I had two lines of credit at that time," he recalls. "It was one of those equal share type of things, where you put in an equal amount of money, then you get an equal share out. So the company paid a portion, and we all individually paid a portion towards everything. In the end, we actually ended up owing money to the company. It was a bit overwhelming, and I felt like I got caught up in a whirlwind, like I didn't have any real input. But then, I didn't even know what kind of input I *could* have. I didn't know what to expect.

"Two of the people who were the heads of the group, so to speak, had done quite a bit of touring for a couple of years, and they knew what to expect. We were learning the ropes from them. Unfortunately, even the best laid plans can go astray; they knew what to expect; they knew what might go wrong; and basically everything that could go wrong, did go wrong. We didn't fail utterly, but we certainly did not do well.

"If I were starting off brand-spankin' new, I would make sure I found out about every aspect of touring from the beginning."

"When you're trying to plan what the heck you're going to bring on tour, if you can, get rid of things, economize, pare things down," advises Charlie. "If you can camp instead of staying in a hotel, do it. It sounds super-cheap, but in the end the dollars and cents really add up.

"Also, for your first time out, I wouldn't go with a huge group of people. It's one of those things where you'll have a fantastic time, you're with a group of people you can share the experience with, but in the end, unless you've already got a whole whack of money saved up, you're going to lose. It's a fact."

"If somebody brings you on for a fringe show, make sure you have some kind of guarantee in writing that you're going to make money every week, even if it's a hundred bucks. It's better than nothing when you're out there; a hundred bucks feels like a million when you've got next to nothing.

"If it's your show and you can, do it by yourself. Even if you're not kicking ass and selling out the theater, in the end, that money is gonna come back. It's gonna pay off your expenses and your overhead, and it's going back in your pocket. Yes, it's good to have someone there, like maybe a stage manager, someone to help share the load—sometimes money can stretch across two people pretty well, and you can still make a dollar.

"I had about nine, ten years of just gigging, going to every little town, doing all kinds of stuff. Nothing really has a through line; you could be doing some eighteenth-century piece here, the next place you're doing a brand-new play, the next, Neil Simon. You don't feel you're actually doing anything, you're not building a career. Now I make a better living by about five or six times touring my own work than I ever did gigging as an actor.

"I'm not trying to overstress the fact that you have to make money. But you don't want to be driven away by financial ruin. You want to be able to keep your head above water, or just barely in the black, so that next year you can, in fact, invest again."

You need to know some of the ways in which festivals compensate performers, writers, and playmakers. This knowledge will help you project the financial future of your project.

- **Nailing down splits.** What kind of financial arrangements do the planners at the fests you'll be working at make with performers? Box-office splits are the most common. There is usually a standard split a venue proposes (say 60/40; you usually get the 40), but sure, you've got wiggle room to negotiate. Keep the following in mind: You must have your split put in writing before you go to a fest if that's the way that festival does business. If they won't back up the promise in ink, scratch the fest off your list.
- **Understanding fixed fees.** Most fringes are going to operate using splits, but what about playwriting festivals and world-renowned performance festivals? Smaller playwriting fests might simply offer a cash prize system and possibly expenses to participating authors. A more prestigious fest is most likely going to work out a fixed fee with participating playmakers, which may or may not include a box-office cut. It's vital that you open discussions to agree upon a fixed fee, plus get your arrangements set in a signed contract. Most well-known fests keep individual artists' financial arrangements confidential, and amounts paid will tend to vary, based on the artist's reputation and experience.

Make sure you plan for all foreseeable production expenses, and certainly be aware of the almost inevitable possibility of unforeseeable expenses.

- **Festival fee.** Do not forget to include this in any budget. Participation in any single festival can cost anything from nothing to hundreds of dollars.
- **Related venue fees.** In some cases, you may have to pay additional fees to your venue. For example, you may have to pay

for specialized SFX costs or specialized equipment rental. You may also have to seek out and arrange the specifics of your own performance space independent of a festival (as is the case with Edinburgh). Get all such fees outlined in writing from the word "go." FYI: Nine times out of ten, all venue fees will be included in the participation fee, but be certain that this is the case.

• **Transport expenses.** Figuring out how you're going to move your sets to your venues isn't just a logistical issue; it's a financial one. I've heard of a number of troupes sending their sets ahead via UPS and FedEx. This may seem to be an extravagant expense at first, but when you really sit down and crunch the numbers, shipping costs can be miniscule in comparison to renting and maintaining a truck. If your set is small enough, it also saves you load-in/load-out headaches—you don't need to employ extra techies.

• **Performance set-up.** At most large fests, you're assigned a fast turnaround set-up time (usually a half-hour to get your set and tech equipment in place, which often happens as the performance before you is completing its strike). You usually get one set-up/strike rehearsal slot before you actually go up. So what could that possibly have to do with your finances, you ask? Plenty, if you violate any rules while setting up (or striking). Many fests level fines against groups that damage either backstage or performance spaces (even for seemingly minor offenses, like if you accidentally chip a little wall paint or leave scuff marks on the stage floor). As far as expensive tech equipment is concerned, rest assured that if you break it, you most likely bought it (talk about a potential budget-buster!). So plan to be careful.

• **Unforeseen venue costs.** If you're late arriving at a venue and delay rehearsal time slots, or, heaven forbid, performance times, venues may try to impose fines or penalties against you. This type of fee, in my mind, is justified. Throwing an entire performance schedule into chaos is just selfish. (Even if you encounter a true emergency en route, you should absolutely

call ahead to avoid such a messy problem.) When are venue costs
not justified? When they're sprung on you at the last minute
after you've arrived. (Suddenly there's an extra insurance fee you
need to take care of, or tech fees that were never previously
discussed and agreed upon, for instance.) Your course of action?
Get everything in writing beforehand, and refuse to perform if
someone attempts to pull the wool over your eyes.

Debts: Real and Imagined

Commercial producers are often turned on to good work by fest
leaders. Why do fest personnel engage in such generous behavior?
Often it's out of sheer desire to help a show move forward to the
next level. Sometimes, however, it's all about getting cut in to
future profits. So what do you really owe a festival in the future if
it puts up your show, and that show gets a commercial pick-up?

It depends largely upon a festival's policies and infrastructure. Many festivals have enough on their plates as is
without getting involved in moving shows to Broadway or the
West End. Fergus Linehan's take: "We had a show we produced
in 2002 that we did in the Royal Court in London and in
Edinburgh. And we had a show that we produced in 2003,
which went to the U.S. in June 2004. We try and get it off our
backs as quickly as possible because we're just not geared up for
it. Effectively, we're a very small operation, and we've become
very big. So we're pretty focused on just getting the projects for
each season up and done.

"But having said that, we help it go. We try to find the right
management for it. The show that we've got at the moment that
we had last year and is doing huge touring now in a way was a bit
easier, because everyone wants to do it. Therefore, the fees are
fine and all the rest of it, and agents are interested in handling it.
But we can't actually get out there and start organizing the freight

arrangements and the flights and start selling it to other festivals or anything like that. We're just not geared up for that."

The director of the Belfast Festival, Stella Hall, believes that in order to move forward, a piece must effectively address universal issues. "What is the quality in a piece of writing or a production that means that it speaks to an audience if it goes to the U.S., or goes to India, as loudly, or nearly as loudly, as speaks to an audience here?' she asks. "It has to do with issues that cross boundaries and affect us all. It's intrinsically about human relationships, friendships, family, personal identity, loss and grief and how one deals with it, how one heals it. So that the writing—although focused on this place—can deal in a way that actually transcends that very specific physical and temporal location."

In a similar vein, Joseph Mellilo of BAM feels that during his tenure, BAM's greatest achievement from both a creative and production business standpoint has been quite universal in scope: "The work on our stage is global, not Euro-centric."

The Humana fest actually schedules in a performance weekend for producers seeking pick-ups. Says Zan Sawyer-Dailey of Humana's intent: "We do want to help these people (festival playwrights) move their plays forward. I would guess we have a very high percentage of the plays that come away with an option. How many of those options get exercised over the next two years is anybody's guess. We had a big, big hit with the play *Omnium Gatherum*—it was just a phenomenal production, and quite the toast of the festival. Usually when you have one big, big, big hit, that means the festival will be a success, because it sort of carries the rest of the plays. On years when nothing seems to soar and they're all pretty solid, the festival sort of doesn't seem to take off as high, so we're always thrilled when at least one play really hits.

"So *Omnium* obviously went into New York. It did well— I won't say that it was quite the commercial success that people thought it would be, but it was not our production. It was optioned by an Off-Broadway producing entity, and that producing team took it in. They used a lot of our cast—we don't have any rights to that. We do get some subsidiary rights—we have some marginal follow-up to these things—but it's not our production."

What arrangement you specifically wish in regard to future profit action should be spelled out clearly in your contract, and should be negotiable. It's fine for a festival to have a standard percentage they take off royalties for a certain length of time—as long as that percentage is not astronomical, and that length of time isn't in perpetuity. But there always needs to be room for negotiation, and a little back-and-forth about the details. You should never do business with an entity that wants to dictate the terms of owning your own property to you.

Often, a festival or production entity will want an "originally produced at or by" credit—ostensibly harmless, right? Well, not really—an originating producer usually has a legal claim to some portion of future royalties FOREVER. And perhaps the "originating producer" you're negotiating with doesn't even deserve that title—if your college roommate helped you stage an initial reading of the piece in the early nineties, technically, HE could be considered the "originating producer." See how complex this can get? That's why, again, you need a good lawyer to look over every single contract you receive, and do the talking and strikeouts for you if need be. The Dramatists Guild can be also be quite helpful in familiarizing novice writers with appropriate percentages, rights, and credits.

Fast Facts to Remember

Here are a number of very important business points to keep in mind when dealing with a variety of situations at and around a festival. Memorize these points, and they'll get you through a tough or confusing on-the-spot scenario.

- Don't feel guilty asking for what you're worth in a negotiating situation. Festivals have corporate sponsors, for the most part; the money is there to pay you (most of the time). Never be arrogant, outrageous, or ridiculous in your demands, but don't be timid, either. Speak up with a best-case scenario— you can always bang out a solid compromise if you have to.

- Unless it's contractually stipulated, you are under no obligation to use the festival director's girlfriend in your production.

- Producers can, however, offer actors from your show the chance to move on to greener pastures by plucking them out of your show and putting them into a new production of your material (should you sign an option). Actors Equity usually makes such transitions easy, as its job is to watch out for the welfare of its members above all else.

- Never try to impress a producer with baloney. You look like an instant mark the second you're caught in a silly fib or spouting inaccurate gossip, and the producer either won't take you seriously or will try to rip you off royally.

- When in doubt, smile and say nothing.

- When a businessperson says something surprising or makes you an offer, say nothing again. Just look at him/her, and chance are the pause in your response will keep him/her chattering. You'll get a bit more essential information by throwing this person off his guard.

- Don't verbally agree to any deal! Even though oral contracts are tough to prove, they DO lead to lawsuits sometimes. Stay noncommittal until you see terms on paper.

The Motion of Promotion

"I've seen wonderful shows that have had terrible promotion," says Jan Munsil (of the Uno Festival). "If I had known how wonderful they would be, I'd have said, 'Listen! You've got to get the word out in a more professional way. You have to present yourself differently, because if you don't everybody's going to miss the show, and it's a wonderful thing.' By the time you get your show up and running, you're so tired, you don't feel you've got the energy for promotion, but it's important."

If you're uncomfortable with the idea of "selling" your art, get over yourself. You already sell your product—your work—every time it goes up on another stage. You sell it by making sure the acting's first-rate, the lighting's good, the script's solid, and the design is effective. Really, extending what you already do under the banner of "promotion" or "marketing" isn't all that much of a stretch.

If you're a theater person, you're probably a people person, to some degree. You may not always turn on the megawatt charm in real life, but your personality skills are well developed. You can definitely "act" the part of a salesperson in order to get the word out about what a good show you have. Your first PR step starts before you leave home: You need to gather good-looking materials for a press kit, and also to hand out promotionally at festivals to potential audience members. At a fringe, groups of patrons waiting to see a show are called "line-ups," and performers routinely work them, handing out postcards and flyers to attract them to upcoming performances and answering questions about their shows.

So what specific type of PR works best? "There is nothing more valuable in the world than good, professional photos," says Jan Munsil. "The fringe is this huge marketplace, and a good photo can land you on the front page of the newspaper. It's really important, and you might go, Oh my God, it's going to cost $200, but that's nothing compared to the amount of publicity you can get. So many of the photos (received at her Fringe) are out of focus, taken with a disposable camera in front of the fireplace with nine people staring cheesily at the camera, making bunny ears behind each other's heads. That is useless. Make that investment! It might be more than the entire budget of your show, but it will really pay off."

Shannan Calcutt agrees. "If you're going to spend money on promotion, I'd say photographs are the way to go," says Shannan Calcutt. "If you have a good color photograph that the press is going to like—a bright photo that's going to get attention—then you're set. There's where I spent my money. I spent a lot of money on them, but I had a fantastic photographer, Gary Mulcahy in Toronto. I got so many photos in the paper because of that. Once you get photos in the paper, that's money made with advertising. You do have to think that way—you have to think with both sides of the brain."

To get those photos in the paper, put them in a press kit package consisting of:

- One great picture, preferably a black and white 8" × 10".
- A press release touting your show and briefly, your credentials. Include all relevant contact and performance information pertinent to each fest you're working at.
- A cover letter stating that you're available for interviews, again, with full contact info.
- Great previous reviews or press write-ups. You'll add new reviews and write-ups as you get them on the circuit.

Mail these packages out about three weeks prior to your first fest performance, and two weeks before, make a follow-up call offering more information to each reporter or news organization you've contacted. Follow up again the week you open, then again during your run if necessary.

As mentioned in chapter 4, you need to budget at least $600 to keep your press kits flowing through the mail. Some of the money should also go to getting inexpensive promo postcards and flyers printed up. At each fest, hand these out to everybody you can; as some performers do, talk to potential audience members in character if that helps you feel more comfortable chatting up your show. You'll also want to trick up a simple but eye-catching program copy (you can do this on your computer, at an Internet café, or at Kinko's) and have copies of it for every performance.

Camaraderie also helps tremendously to get the word out. "Often you'll put your programs or flyers on the seats in other people's venues before the shows," says Calcutt. "People will recommend your show in their programs. You help each other out a lot—it's the most supportive environment that I've found, where you want other people to be selling out, you want other people to do well."

Tips for Self-Promotion

- Always return phone calls from the press, no matter how small and insignificant the paper might seem. Any potential press mention looks good and gives you momentum.

- See every show you can to gauge the quality of a festival's overall offerings.

- Compliment your competitors' work when it's good. Also, watch the audience carefully to see what its members really appear to think about what they've paid good money to see.

- Don't let blown smoke cloud your vision. When your show's been favorably received, everybody wants to be your friend. Be your own best friend first so you won't need the world's approval, and you'll be able to clearly detect what your "fans" might truly want from you.

- Print some neat-looking business cards up on the computer, and hand one to every single person you meet. This isn't Alex P. Keaton–like; it's professional. Networking is a waste of time unless you practice it properly, and you want the right people to get back in touch with you.

- Are you a "busker"? What's a "busker," anyway? It's a street performer, and fringes are packed with them. If you travel the circuit in this manner, look at your livelihood from the most professional perspective possible: Follow all fest rules, don't harass or stalk passersby, and put out a clean, tall, fat jar for donations. Be charming and do your best work, just as you would on a festival mainstage.

- Don't criticize other playmakers' work to a producer, fellow artist, festival administrator, audience member, or critic—ever. It makes a hideous impression—you look petty and insecure.

Stay positive in your dealings with everyone. Yes, you have to watch your back, but you shouldn't assume every person you meet is going to stab you in it. Put out good vibes yourself, treat everyone you meet and work with fairly and honestly, and hope you're treated the same in return. If you're not, don't stick around for seconds. Remember what that great thinker Maya Angelou once said (and I'm paraphrasing): Once people show you who they are, believe them.

6

Using Feedback in Your Favor

Praise. Criticism. Love. Hate. Everything in between. It's all feedback, and to a smart, savvy playmaker, it's all good (even when it's bad). Every seasoned professional understands the value of reading reviews, listening to audience commentary, and taking in suggestions of advice from theatrical veterans and peers. You have to put earmuffs on that vulnerable little ego of yours to truly get the most out of constructive commentary at times, sure. But if you're serious about making your work the best it can be, you know better than to take a critique personally.

A festival context provides you with the chance to employ feedback to your advantage more effectively than almost any other theatrical setting. The first reason for that is the developmental component—as many fests' intention is to facilitate on-site workshopping, the opportunity exists for playwrights to soak in the best structural and creative expertise possible. Another key plus: The encouragement of the experimental at many fests infuses playmakers with a sense of supportive possibility, and that can allow them to do their very best work.

Additionally, so many festivals have an intricate and effective system for gauging audience opinion; you get the chance to take in a huge cross-section of input from very diverse demographics; and ultimately can choose to address specific points that consistently keep coming up if you want to.

This chapter will help you get the most out of critical, artistic, and patron commentary about your material. It's important to understand when to take ideas seriously, and when not to. It's also vital to maneuver the concept of on-site play development very, very carefully. Though wonderful in theory, and totally productive when a fest handles it the right way, on-site development could also conceivably make your play a disastrous hodgepodge of too many careening, crashing, conflicting contributions. You also have to tread lightly in terms of getting the most out of good *and* bad reviews as your material evolves further. So here's how to watch, learn, and listen most effectively.

Attitude Is Everything

As a playmaker, the basic thing to grasp about feedback and criticism is that no matter how much of it you're confronted with, you ultimately control it. How do you do this? By simply deciding how you're going to react to it, as a rule, and sticking to that rule. You can literally say to say yourself, "I originated this material, so whatever this review says, I know best." Even the opinion of a superb critic like Ben Brantley is subjective, after all. You have to maintain confidence in your vision and statement at all costs in order to have the strength to take your play as far as it can go.

It also helps to see each performance as an individual adventure. Each performance experience is going to be different, good or bad, and will leave you wiser no matter what happens. Shannan Calcutt has mastered this concept beautifully. "As far as the audience goes, with Izzy, the first time I took her out, she was kind of a baby clown, with *Burnt Tongue*, the first show," she recalls. "With the second show, I guess (I was) getting more confident with her and the choices, and really just, myself, getting out of the way and letting her do the show.

"The second show has a lot more audience interaction—having the courage to bring more people onstage and letting them affect your show more, because of course you never know what you're going to get when you ask someone a question. Instead of this being a scary thing, of people going, 'Oh, I don't want to come, I might be brought onstage,' people were actually coming more and more often. They'd want to see the show more than once, because they wanted to see how Izzy would deal with the audience this time, or how it would change the show. So it actually became something that made the show stronger and more desirable to an audience, which was wonderful as well.

"My third show is definitely the most dangerous and brave of them all. I enter the show topless, I have seven wedding dresses onstage, and I'm covering myself with my bag, but the gag, you know, picking up a dress, putting down the bag, that kind of thing. But then she does stand there, reveals herself, and says, 'I want someone to see me just like this and not freak out.' It's a wonderful show in that it is very dangerous; she's right out there, she's extremely vulnerable. And again, Izzy's always able to really take the piss out of herself and laugh at herself; I think people in laughing at her are laughing at their own ridiculousness as well. She takes things to the extreme, you can laugh at them, and I think that's part of her appeal.

"The themes are very universal. Her desire to be loved, rejection she's dealing with all the time, wanting someone to think you're special—all these things are universal. People laugh and cry during the shows—men and women—and I think it's very much a mirror effect. Her vulnerability and playing the emotions to the extreme allows people to see themselves in her.

I think that's the clown's job—to remind us we're all just human, and we shouldn't take ourselves so seriously.

"It's the instant feedback, right there. In clown, you want to take the audience into your world. You're having this experience together. In the first show, I'm waiting for a blind date, and if there's a latecomer, I look at the door—*everyone* looks at the door! It's quite wonderful."

Shannan's experience speaks volumes about the benefits of being in the moment, and developing the right stage self-assurance. Just as that strong self-assurance is so necessary, on the other hand, it's essential to curb an tendency you might have to be a little . . . well, elitist. Even though you *are* the master of your own creative ship, you absolutely don't know everything. If, for example, you go into a symposium environment giving off a snooty, self-satisfied, beret-wearing vibe, the audience is going to be totally turned off. Word of mouth will spread about what an arrogant jerk you are, and your show attendance will drop off. And you'll never get quality feedback from a crowd that thinks you patronize or loathe.

"If you're engaging people in a conversation, you're much more likely to get them to see something extreme and not be frightened by it," says Charles Fee (artistic director and producer of both the Great Lakes Theatre and Idaho Shakespeare Festivals). "Which is, of course, the point of our work—to engage the audience, not to alienate them. There's been an awful lot of that as an issue for us in the theater, and we see it within many communities.

"Some audiences have been alienated by the theater companies themselves, and I think as harsh as that may sound, some of that has been the fault of our focus, because from the late eighties through the nineties, we focused on the auteur concept of the artist. The artists as the sole author of the work and the artists as intellectually remote from the audience. I remember early in my career going to a talkback with a director whose work I really loved. The director's there, okay, with the dramaturg, and here's the audience, eager to talk about this insane production that we'd just watched. I mean, it was just a super-postmodern piece that the audience was completely baffled by. The audience asked him some question about the play, like, you know, 'Why did you have a cow hanging from the tree in that scene?' That was literally the question. And the director's response was, literally, 'Why not?'. And, you know . . . fine, but why come out in front of the audience, then? The audience member now feels like, 'Oh, I must be an idiot,' or, 'Wow, he won't even give me the time of day.' What on earth are we doing this for, then? How can you not be able to engage the audience in some level of discussion if you're a theater artist?

"My advice to my company and the directors when we do these talkbacks is, You've just got to be honest with them. If somebody asks you why you hung the cow in the tree, you may not know. Fair enough. You don't always know. You've just got to look at them and say, 'I've got to admit to you—I can't articulate it. I don't know. Did you hate it? What did you think of it? What did you think it meant?' As long as you're willing to be open with them, audiences will engage in anything, but what they don't want is our sense of being removed from them."

How Many Cooks Should Stir the Broth

If you're toiling at a festival that specifically solicits material with a view toward developing it, a certain amount of cooperative acquiescence is going to be expected of you. This is not always a bad thing: "Feedback is everything!" says Jason Teeter of the Rainbow Theater Festival. "When theaters/performers don't take into account the opinions of the audience or their director, then what they're doing is something quite similar to masturbation.

As artistic director (and actor, director, and playwright within the company), I consistently try to take the pulse of the audience and my peers."

See, that's the right balance to strike: Being open to incorporating good ideas that come your way. However, many artists, playwrights participating in writers' festivals in particular, can become overwhelmed by the pressure to change their work that comes from fest personnel, like dramaturgs. Now, lots of dramaturgs are simply great: experienced in what makes good craft and structure, tactful in offering tips and opinion, mindful of preserving a writer's intent. A few dramaturgs, however, can be domineering and intimidating. They'd rather pontificate about why they know more than you do, how their viewpoint is fresh and highly skilled, and why you should simply give in and accept the fact that they're going to rewrite your play whether you like it or not.

When faced with such a situation, your loyalty should be to your material, *not* the festival, simply because the organization is giving you a coveted chance to present your work. Don't be too grateful for that—your talent is the real object of value here, and any fest would be lucky to have it. No need to flamethrow your way out of a dramaturgical disagreement, however. If you're feeling pressured to alter your work in a manner that's not comfortable for you, simply say to the dramaturg, "I think a lot of what you're saying is valid, but having developed this work for so long, I have very firm reasons why I don't want to change certain things." Then don't change them. If the dramaturg continues to make life difficult, speak to the literary manager, or a fest producer or director higher up. Most likely, the situation will be settled easily; worst-case scenario, this isn't the fest for you, and you'll just have to go elsewhere.

When you're dealing with a number of fest personnel who all have different ideas about what your script should be, you must protect your work from becoming incomprehensible goulash.

Decide which person's opinion is of the most value to you, and listen primarily to this person—maybe it's the artistic director, maybe it's an associate producer. As a rule, it's most likely going to be a person whose position dictates the distinct voice of the festival (since that voice is, no doubt, a main reason you chose to work here in the first place). You can very subtly indicate to others around you that you're in sync with this particular person by addressing your comments about the script in a group meeting to that person, and agreeing very clearly with him on script points in front of others. Most likely, your hint will be taken, and others will back off.

The best fests avoid the problem of conflicting feedback by structuring a system that's beneficial to the playwright's needs (which of course will ultimately result in the best script possible). Says Kim Peter Kovac (co-head of the Kennedy Center New Visions, New Voices Festival), "As you know, feedback comes in many forms. Certainly, there is the talkback session following the reading itself. A lot of times, though, much more is learned in the rehearsal room.

"These days, we have one discussion leader-facilitator who conducts a half-hour session following each reading. The person who's done it most is Todd London, artistic director of New Dramatists in New York. Peter Brosius led discussions one year; Ricardo Kahn will lead them this year. This is a format that has evolved and we're pretty happy with the present format, rather than a panel of talking heads. Most of the audience is intelligent and knows the field, so the leader facilitates their comments. The discussion is geared toward what the playwright and director feel is feedback that they need.

"Other feedback, informally, can come from the festival's dramaturgs. Since these are works in progress, we don't feel it appropriate to assign a dramaturg, student or otherwise. We do have two dramaturgs around during the week of New Visions, and the teams are free to use them as a resource. Past dramaturgs have included Lenora Inez Brown, Mary Hall Surface, Michael Lupu, and Laurie Brooks."

The Power of Buzz

"There's a unique kind of bond, really, between a performer, audience, and critic here at Edinburgh," says Paul Gudgin, "in that with 1,500 shows, the audience has a hell of a job deciding what to go and see. The way most people choose what to go and see is really twofold: One is by reading reviews, and the second is by talking to other members of the audience. What we call "the grapevine" in Edinburgh is unbelievably fast and largely sophisticated. Basically, if there's a good show out there, people will find out about it fairly quickly, and it is fascinating; a show can really get a buzz going on it, and people find out about it, and they end up filling it.

"Part of that is the role of the critic, which I think is more important in Edinburgh than in most other places. A good review equals bums on seats in Edinburgh, generally. But also, this frustrating thing, I think, particularly for publicists because they can't really influence it easily, is this whole idea of word of mouth, of people talking about shows, the word going around that there's a good show somewhere. In some ways, it's not a matter of performers sitting down at the end and saying to the audience, 'What do you think of our show'?' To be honest, it's much more immediate than that. The audience is telling them what they think of their show by talking about it and coming to it.

"There are always frustrations, and there are always very good shows that somehow don't ever quite seem to get that buzz for whatever reason. Also, there are some shows where they've just spent a lot of money on them, and they've been marketed well, which aren't very good shows, but are still getting the audiences. But on the whole, the whole sort of audience grapevine and review infrastructure of the Fringe does tend to see the cream rise to the top."

It's really true—once the word gets out, it's hard to keep a good show down. If you're getting deluged with positive comments, that's absolutely fantastic, and a real credit to the job you've done with your production. Obviously, things are working. That's not to say you should feel you can never again tinker with your material, though. If some little nagging point at the top of Act Two is bothering you, by all means, fix it as you see fit.

If word of mouth is less than stellar, however, and you feel the bad buzz is confirming fears you've had about parts of your show, the perfect solution may be to use the audience's points in making major repairs. Sabrina Hamilton (artistic director of Ko Fest) shares her company's uniquely effective audience feedback system: "Every single show has a lobby display. Every lobby display contextualizes Ko and its history, but then it contextualizes the piece. I always tell people to bring anything they threw out of the production. Any prop, any of the research. So we do a lobby display of that, and after the show, we always have facilitated discussions, after every single performance. Sometimes, the discussions have even been longer than the shows!

"The feedback is not always about the work; sometimes we specifically ask for that. Because we don't just open the show and leave it at that; they (the artists) can go in and rehearse the next day, and sometimes take the audience feedback and incorporate it right into the performance."

That's the great thing about festivals: Oftentimes, you can put an adjustment immediately on its feet and see how it feels, and plays. If a change the audience has suggested to you doesn't work, or simply doesn't feel right, by the same token, you can certainly scrap it. Again, it all goes back to you—what you think and intend for your project must be the driving factor. Joseph Melillo of BAM weighs in: "We have an audience that desires to hear the originating artist(s) talk about their work." Your audience should be willing to respect your thoughts on your work first and foremost, even if members of that audience or (ghastly a prospect it may be) the whole lot doesn't love what you've done.

Also, it always helps to work with a festival that's got a good feel for what its audience might be engaged in, and is thoughtful in terms of both passing that info along to its artists, as well as programming smartly. Fergus Linehan takes this point of view: "Obviously one does the research and all of that, but the public will never tell you what they want to see. It's too subtle a seduction, and it doesn't work, actually. We've had the research saying they want to see Shakespeare, and then you do Shakespeare and they don't want to see it. So it's completely instinctive. You just know the audience and you know what they can take. You recognize things that are in competition with each other.

"And then you're looking at dynamics such as, if you know something is really wonderful but it won't have an immediate, obvious appeal to the audience, you know you're going to have to run it a little longer—because it's gonna take a few days for word to get out about what this is. No matter how much you talk about it and how much you hype it, that will only get you so far. So there's kind of logistically, how you plan that out. And also, you've got the media in there a well. You know you have to engage the media in a fairly broad way. One of the things about festivals that's really useful is they get the arts off the arts page and onto the front page."

Critical Conditions

They say that there's no such thing as bad publicity. Still, what a critic may think about your production can have impact on the fate of a show—in some situations, lots more than others. A Broadway show with an all-out pan from the *Times*, for instance, probably isn't going to take up permanent residence in Shubert Alley.

The good news for you, though, that in the average festival setting, a bad review isn't going to wipe you out. The reason for this? Quite bluntly, yours isn't the only show in town. You're playing as one production among a roster of many, and usually, just one or two full-on smashes will emerge. If your show doesn't happen to be one of them, you can play out your run, then take some downtime to analyze the critical feedback you've gotten to see if you might want to change and restage your piece.

Of course, good reviews can help a show in spades on the fest circuit. In addition to staging a quality production, you can actually increase your chances of positive critical mention by working at a fest that has a nice relationship with news outlets. Jon Tuttle, literary manager of Trustus, says, "I think the Trustus Festival is treated very fairly and quite well by the local media. There are typically two or three newspaper critics there on opening night—and they have high expectations. Not always have their reviews been positive, but they *usually* are, and when they're not, they offer some useful insights. There's also some good, front-page-of-the-Arts-section preview material the week before the opening. Television coverage is hit-or-miss, depending upon the size of the news hole that week. This past year, we got a nice preview article in *American Theatre* magazine for Sarah Hammond's *Kudzu*, and intend to sustain that relationship now that we have it."

When you collect a favorable notice, know what to do with it: Walk it straight over to the nearest copy machine. Update all your press kits with copies, then hand out reviews to anybody you think should have one: audience members in line-ups, producers, fest personnel, fellow artists you want to collaborate with. Mail out copies to more reviewers to demonstrate your heat and hopefully, attract them to the show. Send them ahead to other fests you will be working at, or hope to work at. Basically, paper the earth with your good news, and odds are interest will roll back your way.

The Ultimate Truth

When you get right down to the nitty-gritty, if you really want to know what a fest audience thinks of your work, check out your house seats. Do you have bodies in them? If so, chances are you've done quality work and people are hearing about it. Says Leah Cooper, executive director of the Minnesota Fringe Festival, in regard to the Minnesota scene: "The Fringe is uniquely democratic in its selection process, and audience-driven in its feedback cycle. There are too many shows and too little time for box office to be driven by reviews from critics. Word of mouth is the driving force in success and feedback for artists. This means artists get the chance to learn, hands-on, how to produce and promote for an audience. Often the impact of creative feedback on artists in the Fringe is that they grow from newbies into successful, sustainable small companies who not only understand how to create theater, but also market and manage it. They also learn just how far they can go to the very outer fringe edges of creativity."

Don't let pride keep you from admitting you need to make improvements, either in your show or your marketing approach. If you hesitate, you'll be swiftly run over by the show behind you on the program—at a large fest or a fringe, there's always gonna be scores of shows that audiences can choose instead of yours. Chris Gibson, executive director of the Orlando Fringe, addresses the high traffic issue: "With the volume of programming that the Orlando Fringe is presenting, we aren't able to offer a forum for direct audience feedback per se. But artists definitely can gauge the validity of their work within our particular arts market based on ticket sales—or lack thereof! Artists whose work is sub-par are of little interest to our community and will not see much in the way of attendance, while those who present high-quality, engaging programming will see a direct response with sold-out houses. Word of mouth is key. The Orlando Fringe fans are notorious for lining up for blocks for that "must-see" show, as well as staying away in droves once the word gets out that a show is a waste of time and/or money. Our most successful returning artists use audience response as a barometer for what works and what doesn't."

The ultimate truth lies in your gut. If you know a particular city isn't getting your show, chalk it up to experience and look forward to the next town. If you know you really should clean things up, or scrap a piece altogether, do it. As long as you give yourself, and your work, your best shot, no festival experience can ever be considered a failure.

7

Staying True to Your Vision

Don't let yourself down.

It's an incredibly easy thing to do, you know. You've been working your brains out, stuffing envelopes with pictures, shouting lines till you're hoarse, counting change to chip in for gas money to get to one more fest in one more town, plus you've got a screaming headache and swollen glands and haven't seen your boyfriend or eaten an actual vegetable in over two months. Who wouldn't want to chuck everything and find out if the Krispy Kreme franchise in your hometown is still hiring?

When conditions get bad, it's easy to abandon your creative vision. Hang in there. Burnout may feel like it's looming, but stick things out through this festival cycle. Then you can take a break and regroup. Perspective is everything, and you don't have any right now, so let's give you a little logic to tide you over.

Go Back to the Beginning

"You forget that the work you've put into it, and the creative process, is the success," says Shannan Calcutt. "Of course, you want to play for a big house, because more people are laughing, same with crying, and yeah, you're going to make more money. But remind yourself why you're there."

There are no guarantees in the business of theater; you know that. Even if you're touring the greatest show on God's green earth, that doesn't mean everyone is going to get your point. But if you keep on working and hear primarily good feedback from one person, then another, then a couple more, you're doing something right. So keep doing it.

Fergus Linehan describes his philosophy regarding his own company and its good advice for any theater pro: "I suppose overall you've got to know yourself. When you've put together a good program and the mix is right—you never really know until you're right in the middle of it. We put a season together in 2001 that was just about as close as I got to getting it absolutely right. Unless you're very close to it, you wouldn't even notice it. People say, 'Yeah, this is a good one, that was a good one,' do you know what I mean? But they don't *really* know the difference."

Respect and trust your original vision, and let it carry you forward.

It's a Marathon, Not a Sprint

"It often doesn't happen in your first year here," says Edinburgh's Paul Gudgin. "I think most people, it often takes them two or three years to build those connections. If you do have the talent, and you have an individual voice, and you have something unique to say, you will be discovered. It is enormously hard work; Edinburgh is all about self-sufficiency. You have to be prepared to go and ring the journalists. People just don't come flocking because you're remarkably talented—you have to get out there and tell people that you're remarkably talented. I think that's a very, very important thing: You have to be willing to put in the work, and you have to be willing to sell what you have. I have to say, for American performers, that seems to come more naturally than it does for their English counterparts! That's one.

"The second thing is not to believe that there's a 'Fringe formula,' necessarily. I think some people sometimes want that success, and they think that the way to achieve it is to look for how it's been achieved and mirror that formula. I'm afraid there isn't a single formula, because if there was I would be making a fortune selling it! What we do is help you avoid the major pitfalls, just telling you what we've seen that works. But at the end of the day, you have to be bright enough to work out what is going to work for you.

"The last thing that I would always say is that I would hate people to be just coming to Edinburgh for 100 percent professional reasons, just to develop their career. Edinburgh is a trade show, but if that's all it was it would be very, very boring. What Edinburgh is much more about is fourteen thousand performers being within the city at one time and actually dominating that city. What I really want is for people to learn from their fellow performers, to enjoy being in their company. To enjoy the fact that they are part of an artistic community that has taken over a city for three or four weeks. I would always say that to performers: Don't come here solely because you want to get that contact, you want to get that gig, you want to get whatever. You've got to come here wanting to be part of that whole artistic community, because I think then you stand a better chance of being successful."

When the going gets tough, focus on the positive: Go see another artist's show, something with great buzz. Then don't sit there feeling envious of the way she connects with and holds the audience's attention better than you do; instead, resolve to rediscover your own work with the same enthusiasm this performer is infused with. Really let yourself feel the excitement of a good show, and you'll want to create the same electricity again.

Try to remember, too, that patience is a virtue for a reason. You're building a career, and that doesn't depend solely on how you do within the context of a single given show or festival. You have to bide your time. Try to do one thing every day to bring you closer to a goal—write a new press release, call that newspaper, or take the time for a good, long brush-up rehearsal. Small, productive steps add up to big dividends.

Seek Out Support

When you're feeling exhausted and creatively misunderstood, go hang out with that friendly associate producer you met in the Fringe office for a while. She saw your show and raved about it; it's perfectly okay, and not selfish in the least, to spend a little time in her company to give your ego a shot in the arm. The best festivals understand that, and are structured to provide their artists with creative reassurance whenever it's required. Stella Hall (Belfast Festival Director) wants her artists to feel they can "take their work to the next level—test themselves in a supportive environment." What could be better? A festival that encourages its audiences to provide positive feedback is incredibly important as well. Such is the case with BAM, where, Joseph Melillo observes, "We have an audience that desires to hear the originating artists talk about their work."

That's key. Sometimes, all you need to do in order to reinvigorate your creative vision within yourself is verbalize a bit about your work. On the fest scene, there are numerous ways to do this: with an audience, which is of course fantastic; with other artists on your peer level, with whom you can build a strong mutual admiration society and support system; and with established artists or fest leaders you look up to, who can offer you guidance, sure, but to whom the simple act of articulating what your show's about can often be very clarifying. Don't isolate yourself—indulge in lots of healthy give-and-take.

Be In the Moment

"When I think about it, that first tour had so many strange things happening," says TJ Dawe. "Like my car, for instance, in the end needed about $1,600 in repairs. Supposedly, if we'd dealt with it early, it would have cost about $25, but I had to keep on driving it. So many things happened on that first tour; no tour since then has been so eventful.

"In a lot of ways, quitting was just never an option. Whenever I'd get to a new city—it was my first tour, so people would never have heard of me, the press would never have heard of me, the staff, the volunteers, the audiences—I was starting fresh. My shows don't have catchy titles; they don't have sex or nudity on the poster or in the title; I've got no hook. I can't describe my show in ten words or less. I'd have to talk to someone for like a minute just to describe the show, and that ended up being my sales schtick, to go on in this long, fast patter that people found really amusing.

"But I'd have to start over again in every city; my first few shows, I'd be playing to audiences of ten or less. My stage manager would come backstage and tell me, 'We've got six people in the audience tonight.' Part of me would go, 'Ah, shit.' Then I'd get out there, and halfway through the show I'd realize I was having the time of my life, and whatever I had to go through for that moment was worth it. Whatever I'd have to go through in the future to get back there would be worth it."

And that sums up just about everything I've covered so far in this book. Loving the experience itself keeps your vision fresh, above everything else.

I think that the most important thing to do on the festival scene is to soak everything in—all of it, every drop of feedback, every accolade, every piece of advice, every cutting comment. Then filter it through your brain, and trust yourself enough only to believe or utilize what makes sense *to you*.

Sure, you may get offered more money than you've ever made in your life to change an intimate solo show in which you poignantly play your great-grandmother as a young girl into a big, schmaltzy, commercial vehicle. It's tempting to alter your initial vision into oblivion in such a situation, but only you know if doing so is truly worth it. It can be wise to make changes, adjustments, and concessions suggested by others—when *they're* wise.

Remember that what's gotten your work this far is your originality, spark, and vitality. Never let some overbearing business type, self-impressed artiste, or nasty critic snuff that out.

Take advantage of every positive development the festival scene brings your way, and use those advantages smartly—to ultimately make the creative statement you want to make. At the end of the day, you have to be able to live with yourself, and your work. Always give your audience, and yourself, the very best you have to offer.

PART 2

The Works Directory

Best New Festival

The following section lists sixty of the world's greatest festivals for fringers, performers, and playwrights, accessible to artists at any stage of their careers, plus another twenty-five terrific honorable mentions. So what constitutes "the greatest" or "the best" festivals, anyway, you're probably thinking?

First off, let me just say that this best-of list, and arguably any best-of list, is utterly subjective in any number of ways. Sure, you may read through the directory and shriek, "Hey, where's that great postmodern-clog-dancing-solo-performance festival I went to last summer? That totally rocked!" I'm sure it did, but there are so many intriguing fests popping up all over the world at any given moment (especially solo performance festivals, usually sans the clog-dancing) that I really had to boil things down.

I selected festivals for inclusion in terms of high artistic quality; strong creative opportunity; diversity of material/artists presented; geographical spread; and potential for growth and profit. I tried to choose festivals that operate with the utmost efficiency and professionalism, festivals that truly love artists and make it easy for them to do their work. Within this directory, you'll find as much specific selection criteria, submission tips, lifestyle vibe, and inside track info as possible. That said, in the festival world, guidelines, requirements, and updated essentials vary and change extremely often. If you're interested in getting involved with any or all of the festivals listed, it's imperative that you check Web sites religiously, e-mail, or call for the most current specifics you need to know (most often regarding housing, fees, and profits).

You'll also find this section peppered with inside nuggets and slice-of-life details about the festivals listed, plus extensive quotes by many personnel who are associated with the fests. May you find success, great collaboration, and fun by using these pages!

Section 1

Fringe Festivals

Adelaide Fringe Festival, Australia

Founded: Early 1970s

Contact Info: Adelaide Fringe Festival, P.O. Box 3242, Rundle
   Mall, ADELAIDE SA 5000 Australia
   +61 (8) 8100 2000 (phone); +61 (8) 8100 2020 (fax)

E-mail: buzz@adelaidefringe.com.au

Web site: *www.adelaidefringe.com.au*

Performance Dates: Biennially, usually from the end of February
   to the middle of March.

The Festival's Mission: This fringe is very big on artistic risk,
   and always has been. Initially, the Adelaide Fringe was created to counteract the perceived vanilla, mainstream programming of a locally competing festival, the similarly
   named Adelaide Festival. Eventually, the two fests merged,
   and have expanded incredibly—the Adelaide Fringe is now
   the second largest fringe on earth (just behind Edinburgh)
   and hosts an astonishingly 850,000-plus audience members
   every two years.

Application Specifics: Visit the Fringe Web site at the above
address for most current information. Most likely, you'll simply e-mail your contact info and the Fringe will be back in
touch when registration officially opens.

Fees: A registration fee, plus you pay all your own performance
costs. Contact the fest to inquire about current amounts charged.

Selection Criteria: This fringe is unjuried and accepts scores of
artists from Europe, the United States, Canada, Australia, and
beyond—literally everyone who registers.

Payments/Profits/Benefits: The Fringe is very helpful in terms
of artist relations. They provide copious written guidelines—on media and marketing, for instance. The amount
of cash you make at the door is strictly dependent upon
how well you promote yourself, though. (They offer only
a listing in the official program and a Fringe-place mention
in the local paper).

Physical Production Details: When you register, you get access to
the Fringe's Artist Bureau staff, who can give you the latest
availability info on spaces. The staff can also hook you up
with already-booked artists in regard to sharing prime space.

FYI: Start communicating with the staff as early as possible, and
read up on local culture—venues are scattered throughout
every corner of Adelaide (from street set-ups to the city
university).

Housing: Not provided, though the Fringe offers written accommodations info to all artists.

Past Artists/Productions of Note: Blast Theory, a multimedia performance group who acted as Fringe "Thinkers in Residence"
in 2004. The group produced a wild audience participation
adventure involving tech equipment (like global positioning
systems) that took participants on a wild trip through the
streets of the city.

Festival Flavor: Surprisingly family-friendly. There's a great day-
long program called Tanata Kurta (Many Place) that focuses

on cultural education, plus a strong emphasis on youth arts education through the Fringe. Plus, the opening Fringe Parade is packed with kids.

The Bottom Line: It's a great place to try out super-experimental performance, and it also provides invaluable international networking opportunities and a chance to showcase your work to scouting producers.

Dublin Fringe Festival, Ireland

Founded: 1995

Contact Info: Dublin Fringe Festival, 12 East Essex Street, Dublin 2 Ireland
+ 353 1 6778511 (phone)

E-mail: fringe@eircom.net

Web site: *www.fringefest.com*

Performance Dates: Annually each fall (traditionally a few weeks in September-October)

The Festival's Mission: To spotlight unique, innovative perform-ance in theater, dance, multimedia, music, and art that is not usually offered in Dublin. This fringe wants its artists to explore new ways of thinking creatively and new routes to inspiration via the festival environment.

Application Specifics: Visit Web site at above address to down-load the latest version of the Fringe application with updated requirements.

Fees: See current application for current requirements.

Selection Criteria: This fringe is curated, and very choosy. If you're not an established artist (either internationally or from Ireland), your chances are nil for acceptance, so amateurs needn't even bother. If, however, you've got some solid pro-fessional credentials under your belt and you prove that your work will push the envelope creatively, your chances are one in three of getting into the festival.

Payments/Profits/Benefits: Inquire about current guidelines
if chosen.

Physical Production Details: Venues include the Abbey and
Peacock Theatres, Andrews Lane Theatre and Studios,
Focus Theatre, the Space @ the Helix Theatre, the Samuel
Beckett Theatre and Players Theatre, Bewleys Café Theatre,
The New Theatre, the Project Arts Centre, Theatre Space
@ Henry Place, plus museum spaces.

Housing: Inquire about availability if chosen.

Past Artists/Productions of Note: Pulitzer Prize winners, like
playwright Nilo Cruz.

Festival Flavor: Fergus Linehan of the Dublin Theatre Festival
is very admiring of his colleagues at the Dublin Fringe. He
points out, "The Fringe here in Dublin is a curated Fringe. It
isn't just as open door, like in Edinburgh. At times they will
kind of help a company out, but not always (in terms of helping a promising show move to the next level). Knowing that
subtle distinction makes all the difference."

The Bottom Line: A prestigious, popular fest (more than 50,000
attendees on average) for highly respected or highly promising cutting-edge artists and companies.

Edinburgh Festival Fringe

Founded: 1947

Performance Dates: Annually for three weeks in August.

Contact Info: Edinburgh Festival Fringe, 180 High Street,
Edinburgh, EH1 1QS Scotland
0131 226 0026 (phone); 0131 226 0016 (fax)

E-mail: admin@edfringe.com

Web site: *www.edfringe.com*

Performance dates: Annually for three weeks in August.

The Festival's Mission: Originally an offshoot of the Edinburgh
International Festival, the world's first fringe began in order to

give performing artists the opportunity to work completely without limits, and to bring their creativity to as many audience members in the area as possible. Known affectionately now as the "Queen Mother," it's the largest arts festival on earth today. (See chapter 1 for more history.)

Application Specifics: See Web site at the above address for a registration form. Fill it out and send it in, and the Fringe will then contact you with more information. The Queen Mother is absolutely fantastic when it comes to providing complete, easy-to-understand info packages—their material includes brochures on venues, safety, marketing, tech, and much more.

Fees: About twelve pounds to register; then to participate, approximately two to three hundred pounds (roughly 400 to 600 American dollars).

Selection Criteria: "We present all 1,500 shows in pretty much the same format," says Paul Gudgin, festival director. "They've all got forty words in our program. The audience—what they know is that there's this fabulous festival happening. What they know is in and amongst the 1,500 shows, there will be some real gems and stuff they will like. The job of the audience is to sort that out, work out what they want to go and see, which means that our audience is working harder than almost any festival audience, to work out what they're going to go and see. Which I think is in some ways liberating; they're not being led by the nose, they're not being told, 'This is a great performance and that is a great performance.' There's no single authority telling you what you should go and see."

Payment/Profits/Benefits: Whatever you can make through ticket sales, but since that average number of 1,500 shows are happening per fest, don't count on much cash.

Physical Production Details: You must seek out and pay for your own venue. The Fringe very helpfully supplies all participants with brochures listing potential spaces, which range in size from fifty to five-hundred-plus seats. Ask the Fringe for lots of help if you need it; if you don't live in Edinburgh and can't get there before the Festival, request specs and contact info for venues. You'll have to book yourself into a space on your own, and negotiate your own space payment as well. Your show must be completely organized, from personnel to tech, before you arrive in Scotland.

Housing: Not provided, but the Fringe is great about providing an accommodation database to help you weed through hostels, hotels, B&Bs, etc.

Past Artists/Productions of Note: Tons, including Emma Thompson, Hugh Grant, David Schwimmer, Rowan Atkinson, Eddie Izzard, Stephen Fry, Hugh Laurie, Richard Eyre, Ruby Wax, Tom Conti, Billy Connolly, Michael Palin—and yes, *Jerry Springer: The Opera* started here. "In 2003, there was a performance called *Ladies and Gentleman* that was basically done in some public toilets," says Gudgin. "Half of the audience went into the ladies' and half went into the gentlemen's. It was two parts of a performance running in two places at the same time, but you just saw them in a different order. So there were two actors who started their piece of the play in the ladies', and then a couple actors in the gentlemen's, and the audience would then swap over. Of course, what was fascinating after was discussing which order, from your point of view, worked the best. Why I liked it: First of all, it was very brilliantly done. Second of all, it's a typically Edinburgh thing, just using an unusual space, and for that space, then, to become a significant part of the performance. It was a very Fringe thing—an interesting, original idea, interesting space, done very well—it was a fairly fascinating experience, sold-out for most of its run." Also, the writer was Gregory Burke— "a potential major force in Scottish playwriting," says Gudgin.

Festival Flavor: "From a performers' point of view, it's a twofold thing, I think, what they are struck by," says Gudgin. "First of all is how competitive the environment is when it comes to the Fringe, by virtue of the fact that there are 1,500 shows all competing for attention from the audience and the press and everything else. Most people who are used to putting on shows do it in a town or a city where there's fairly limited competition. The audience is nowhere near as big, of course, but there's limited competition—they're competing against five, six, maybe ten things in their locality at any one time. In Edinburgh, you are competing against 1,500 shows, so I think that competition daunts people.

"By the same token, I think the other thing that people are enormously stimulated by is how cooperative it is at Edinburgh. How prepared other performers are to give you the benefit of their advice and their support, and just help each other out. For example, we had a meeting of our principal venue managers last week, and about twenty venue managers came along. There were two people who came along who were completely new, who were just looking to have a venue this summer. Now, basically, they are setting up, as you like, in opposition—they're competitors to the other people who were there. But actually, when we left them in the bar at the end of the evening, the existing venue managers were all crowding around the new venue managers advising them about what they should do, how they should set things up. I think that's entirely part of the spirit of what happens here."

The Bottom Line: The coolest fringe on earth—bar none.

Edmonton Fringe Festival

Founded: 1982
Contact Info: 10330-84th Ave., Edmonton, AB T6E 2G9 Canada
    (780) 448-9000 (phone)
E-mail: fta@planet.eon.net
Web site: *www.fringe.alberta.com*
Performance Dates: Annually for ten days in August.

The Festival's Mission: Initially, the Edmonton Fringe's intent was to model itself on the Edinburgh Fringe's time-tested formula: to give any artist who wanted it the chance to perform without limits, and to make this art available and affordable to as many local folks as possible. The idea was a smash— Edmonton was Canada's first fringe, and today is its biggest, at 450,000-plus audience capacity annually.

Application Specifics: Contact fest at above address or by e-mail for most current guidelines.

Fees: Inquire about current requirements.

Selection Criteria: Unjuried, so anything goes. In 2003, over a thousand performers acted, danced, juggled, recited poetry presented multimedia, and more; genres ranged from classical to super-experimental.

Payments/Profits/Benefits: Inquire about current guidelines.

Physical Production Details: Performances are assigned to indoor venues or on outdoor stages. Buskers fill the streets at will and at random. There's also a "Bring Your Own Venue" system.

Housing: Not provided.

Past Artists/Productions of Note: *Theodore and the Cosmonaut: Love Letters From the Unabomber; Three Dead Trolls in a Baggie; Tranny, Get Your Gun! (Guys in Disguise)*.

Festival Flavor: This fest is huge. Repeat: HUGE.

The Bottom Line: Standing out at such a gathering may be quite a challenge, but the vibrant experience is a must-have, and you can network for days.

Minnesota Fringe Festival

Founded: 1994

Contact Info: 528 Hennepin Ave., Suite 503, Minneapolis, MN 55403
(612) 872-1212 (phone), (612) 871-3460 (fax)

E-mail: info@fringefestival.org

Web site: *www.fringefestival.org*

Performance Dates: Ten days each August, usually spanning the first two weeks of the month.

The Festival's Mission: Executive director Leah Cooper guides this unjuried fringe to present diverse types of live stage performance—upwards of 150 groups perform annually.

Application Specifics: Applications become available during the fall of each year; check Web site, call, or e-mail for annual details.

Fees: The average application fee is $375. This fringe has a graduated fee scale, meaning that artists who require bigger venues and more tech equipment access will pay more than those doing smaller productions.

Selection Criteria: This fringe is open anyone, on a first-come, first-serve basis. Leah Cooper does, however, have a few thoughts on what factors make material "fringey" to the max: "Originality; risk-taking new artists; veteran artists trying new things; genre-defying style; (work that is) challenging to audiences; essential, bare-bones theater—simple set, costumes, and props. Work that focuses on raw performance."

Payments/Profits/benefits: "A low application fee with a 70 percent share in the box office, and expensive items like venue, box office, promotion, and tech handled by the festival means most companies can easily cover expenses," says Cooper. "Financial risks are low, so artistic risks can be high."

Physical Production Details: The Fringe's twenty venues are grouped in a "campus" setting around the downtown, uptown, Lyn-Lake, Powderhorn, and Loring Park sections of Minneapolis. Venues are matched up via application info in regard to stage size and production specifics; assignments are also subject to the order in which applications are received, so the early bird definitely will get the worm. Cooper also notes, "Shows are restricted to ten minutes of set-up and strike time, so production elements have to remain simple."

Housing: Not provided.

Past Artists/Productions of Note: *Around the World in a Bad Mood*, Rene Foss's production about the downside of being a flight attendant, is the highest-grossing show in the festival's history, with receipts topping $10,000. Rewritten into a one-woman piece, the show went on to a smash run in New York, became a successful touring show, and was adapted into a book.

Eating Dreams was created by the students of a high school in Kansas; it was about what was really going on in the minds of contemporary teenagers, and it was staged in an abstract yet confrontational style. Cooper also cites work by the Ministry of Cultural Information, which has grown into a dominant force on the Twin Cities art scene, and the Scrimshaw Brothers, who are adept and wildly popular cabaret performers, as Fringe favorites.

Festival Flavor: *"Voices in the Head* was a late-night show that played every night of the Fringe in 2003," recall Cooper. "The cast was different every night, and was made up almost entirely of performers from other fringe shows who showed up and were cast ten minutes before the show started. Performers each wore headsets connected to DVD players. At the beginning of the show, they all clicked play, and each performer's DVD gave them different instructions, which they followed using improvisation. The entire show came together differently each night into a wonderfully synchronized, but spontaneous, event."

The Bottom Line: A colorful, adventurous, well-attended fringe, staffed by terrifically helpful, friendly folks.

Montreal Fringe Festival (St-Ambroise Montreal Fringe Festival)

Founded: 1982

Contact Info: C.P. 42013, Succursale Jeanne-Mance, Montreal, PQ H2W 2T3 Canada

(514) 849-3378 (phone); (514) 849-5529 (fax)

E-mail: fringe@montrealfringe.ca

Web site: *www.montrealfringe.ca*

Performance Dates: The most recent festival was held
June 10–20, 2004.

The Festival's Mission: This highly respected, unjuried fringe presents work performed in both French and English. "Our next
challenge is to seriously penetrate the francophone audience,"
comments Patrick Goddard, former festival manager. "'Fringe'
doesn't easily translate into French, and it's been a long haul getting the concept out to the media." In 2003, the Fringe pushed
forth in this direction by presenting work in the two spaces of
one of the most prestigious francophone theatres in Montreal,
Theatre d'Aujourd'hui, which impressed many credibility-wise.

Application Specifics: Shows are accepted via a lottery system.
Generally, the first seventy shows to apply get a slot. This
fringe maintains a minimum quota system as well, which
breaks down as follows: 25 percent international companies,
25 percent Canadian (except for Quebec), 25 percent
Quebec anglophone, 25 percent francophone. There's also
a waitlist, which a number of groups do indeed get plucked
per festival. See Web site for latest application info.

Fees: A $20 administration fee for everyone, then a fee per pro-
duction. The amount depends upon the length of your show.
(Latest info is on the application form.)

Selection Criteria: None, but in recent years this fringe has had a
bit of an image makeover from "'amateur' or 'student' festival
to largely 'emerging professional' festival," says Patrick
Goddard, former fringe manger. This is largely due to the fact
that established artists now routinely use the festival to debut
new works (a key example being the prestigious Les Ballets
Jazz de Montreal).

Payments/Profits/Benefits: Each company sets its own ticket price
(up to $9) and keeps 100 percent of the door. A small cus-
tomer service charge may be added by the Fringe.

Physical Production Details: Goddard explains, "We use nine or ten different venues, each configured differently to house six or seven shows over the festival. House seats range from 50 to 115. Stage dimensions are 10' X 10' to maybe 30' X 20'. Lighting and sound is kept as simple as possible, using house equipment if it's available (i.e., if we're renting a year-round theater) or renting a simple dimmer and board system if we're converting a loft or storefront or sculpture gallery. Companies get a max of three hours in the space before their first show—we send them floor plans well before and they are told to keep their lighting and sound simple. Each venue has a house tech who runs the board."

Housing: Not provided.

Past Artists/Productions of Note: TJ Dawe's *Labrador* from 1999, a fanciful tale about touring in Canada; *girlsgirlsgirls*, a sellout in 2000 from director Peter Hinton and writer Greg MacArthur, which Goddard lauds as a "kick-ass verbal and physical show about a group of teenagers who murder a teenage girl"; *JOB: The Hip-Hop Musical*, which is heading Off-Broadway; and *Inconnu 'a cet adresse*, a 2003 piece from Paris set in Nazi Germany about friendship and betrayal.

Festival Flavor: "Feedback is given very directly by audience members through what we call 'Buzz of the Beer Tent'—little review forms that are posted near the box office for the public to see," says Goddard. "Montreal is probably the most fun, social fringe," says TJ Dawe. "Montreal is a really active cultural city—you're probably gonna stay out till 5:00 A.M.!"

The Bottom Line: If you feel your work would translate well in a bicultural setting (or if you happen to work in French), you can't do better than this creatively rich environment.

New York International Fringe

Founded: 1997

Contact Info: Fringe NYC Applications c/o The Present Company, 520 Eighth Avenue, Suite 311, New York, NY 10018

(212) 279-4455 (phone)

E-mail: info@FringeNYC.org

Web site: *www.fringenyc.com*

Performance Dates: Sixteen days annually each summer.

The Festival's Mission: Elena K. Holy, the producing artistic director of the Present Company theatre, started Fringe NYC with her colleagues John Clancy, Nancy Walsh, and Joe Henry Shallenburger, when Clancy questioned the wisdom and expense of touring their company's work to the Edinburgh Fringe. Why travel across the globe to gain buzz in your own hometown, he reasoned? From that initial impetus, the festival has committed itself to spotlighting the best emerging theater artists and productions in the world.

Application Specifics: If you think you've got what it takes, consult the Web site at above address for an updated application. You'll fill that in and mail it along with a cover letter describing yourself and your work, your script/project proposal, a videotape of your work, artist bios of your colleagues on the project, and audiotape or CD of the score if it's a musical project.

Fees: A non-refundable $40 application fee. If you're accepted, you'll also be required to pay a $400 participation fee. International companies also must pay Visa application fees of roughly $150 per group.

Selection Criteria: A very competitive screening process is used to accept work. FringeNYC chooses artists and companies with a view toward a variety of diverse work from all sections of the globe, plus encourages quality work that's brand-new and untested (and that will spark intense artist/audience feedback).

Payments/Profits/Benefits: For every $15 ticket FringeNYC sells to a show, its company receives $8.75. All companies (and in some cases, their authors) must agree to give FringeNYC 2 percent of their gross revenues over $20,000 for seven years of future productions.

Physical Production Details: Approximately twenty Lower East Side venues house all FringeNYC productions, ranging widely from a church off Washington Square Park to Off-Broadway spaces like the Greenwich House Theatre. All tech must be kept extremely simple—each company gets just one cue-to-cue tech rehearsal in space.

Housing: Not provided, but FringeNYC does try to help companies secure cheap accommodations.

Past Artists/Productions of Note: A stellar list, including the Broadway smash *Urinetown: The Musical*, a triple Tony-winner; *Debbie Does Dallas*, which moved Off-Broadway to the Jane Street Theater; *21 Dog Years: Doing Time @ Amazon.com*, which moved Off-Broadway to the Cherry Lane Theatre; plus scores of additional Off- and Off-Off Broadway hits, touring shows, and published plays.

Festival Flavor: Often described as the theatrical equivalent of the Sundance Film Festival. It's daring, it's fiercely independent in its vision, and it garners lots of media ink.

The Bottom Line: Opportunities abound to lure commercial producers here. That, plus its terrific creative track record, makes FringeNYC one of the best.

Orlando International Fringe Festival

Founded: 1992

Contact Info: Christopher Lee Gibson, festival producer/Beth Marshall, associate producer, Orlando Fringe, 398 W. Amelia St., Orlando, FL 32801

(407) 648-0077 (phone)

E-mail: producer@orlandofringe.com

Web site: *www.orlandofringe.com*

Performance Dates: Ten days annually in May.

The Festival's Mission: Officially: "To provide an accessible, affordable outlet that draws diverse elements of the community together and inspires creative experiences through the arts."

FYI: Orlando was the first U.S. fringe, and includes an average of 500 presentations, including stage performances, concerts, a huge parade called the Fringe Frolic, and kids' programming.

Application Specifics: See Web site for latest details.

Fees: See Web site for latest details.

Selection Criteria: This fringe is unjuried, and work is accepted strictly on a lottery basis. (on average, 50 companies perform per festival). Gibson elaborates: "Style, content, and subject matter of presented pieces are not our concern. We simply provide a platform for artists to present their work and for audiences to judge what work has value."

Payment/Profits/Benefits: Inquire about latest guidelines.

Physical Production Details: Venues sprawl across the streets of downtown Orlando.

Housing: Not provided, but the Fringe typically works out discount packages with local hotels. Contact the fest to inquire, or see what's listed on the Web site's home page.

Past Artists/Productions of Note: Gibson doesn't play favorites when it comes to specific productions or artists. "The Fringe is part of a process for artists, and often a very early part of the process. I respect and admire every artist who is brave enough to express himself in front of an audience—not matter what his level of experience or expertise, his style or message. To be an arts patron is to accept the richest reward that life offers you."

Festival Flavor: Devoted festival attendees are notorious for spreading buzz about what shows are good or bad to first-time attendees, so be at the top of your game. "It is a good time, but there's fewer touring shows, because it's out of the (Canadian) loop," says TJ Dawe. "A lot more commercial sensibilities to the shows—I find that a lot of the American shows are a lot more plugged in to pop culture. It's a cultural mishmash, it's sort of the deep South, sort of not. There are a lot of churchgoing people there, and the theater community is quite related to the amusement park industry. There is a strong local scene, but kind of with a commercial bent. Really good people—enthusiastic volunteers and good audiences!"

The Bottom Line: A heavily attended fest that's well regarded by veteran fringe circuit performers.

Ottawa Fringe Festival, Canada

Founded: 1997

Contact Info: The Ottawa Fringe Festival, 2 Daly Avenue, Studio 100, Ottawa, ON K1N 6E2 Canada

(613) 232-6162 (phone); (613) 232-2931 (fax)

E-mail: fringe@ottawafringe.com

Web site: *www.ottawafringe.com*

Performance Dates: Annually in June for approximately nine days.

The Festival's Mission: This unjuried fringe was founded on the principle that the nature of an artist's work shouldn't be judged by anyone other than the artist himself. This philosophy has allowed international and Canadian performers of every stripe to present their statements totally unfettered.

Application Specifics: Eight separate applications are available via the Fringe's Web site, specific to the type work you want to do and the way you want to do it. Prospective Fringers fill out the application that's appropriate, plus a corresponding contract.

Fees: Read specific, updated information included with the individual applications on the Web site.

Selection Criteria: A lottery system is used to determine festival spots.

Payments/Profits/Benefits: 100 percent of the box office is returned to each company.

Physical Production Details: A sampling of venues: the World Exchange Plaza; the Lookout Bar; the Ottawa City Registry

Office; the 4th Stage, National Arts Center; and more. Participants can also bring/create their own venues throughout the city by applying to do so.

Housing: Not provided.

Past Artists/Productions of Note: Recent award-winning Fringers include well-known storyteller John Huston, Sossy Productions out of Minneapolis (which presented *Trick Boxing*, a festival favorite) and Independent Auntie Productions (its show *Clean Irene and Dirty Maxine* took the 2003 Outstanding Performance citation).

Festival Flavor: Audiences here are loyal, and have a taste for adventurous offerings.

The Bottom Line: Well worth the trip!

Philadelphia Fringe Festival

Founded: 1997

Contact Info: Philadelphia Fringe Festival, 211 Vine Street, Philadelphia, PA 1910
(215) 413-9006 (phone)

E-mail: deborah@pafringe.org (to reach program director Deborah Block)

Web site: *www.pafringe.com*

Performance Dates: Annually in September.

The Festival's Mission: Founder Nick Stucchio recalls that he and choreographer/performance artist Eric Schoefer were inspired to start this fringe after a great experience in Edinburgh in 1996. "It was total immersion, first of all. I think we did it the right way. The synergy is amazing. We produced, so I got to actually mount a show within the Fringe, which was a great experience—I learned a lot. As well, I got to talk to the organizers and producers and sort of had a macro-view at the same time. So we basically took the notion of 'festival time'— the environment, the unusual context—we took those ideas and we wanted to build from them here, in our festival. What we did was, we basically established a festival we called 'fringe,' and we meant the term to sort of recreate the fun, interesting context, and about the work, about the sort of experimental, contemporary art that we loved. We wanted to use the term 'fringe' in that meaning, not in the meaning of 'unjuried.'"

Application Specifics: Simply e-mail the Fringe at the above address and describe yourself and your work. This festival is curated, but very focused on innovation, so emerging artists definitely stand a chance (see Selection Criteria below). The staff will be back in touch with you, and if your work sparks interest, they'll ask you to send more info and material.

Fees: None.

Selection Criteria: "We built the Fringe on two platforms," says Stucchio. "One is a platform that is juried and selected, because for me, if we relied on the system of a lottery or first-come, first-served, that's a bias against artists who just aren't very good administratively, and we would never see some excellent work. And then we do a sort of homage to the wonderful adventure of the true Fringe spirit, which is about non-curation and self-presentation and anybody having a chance. We call that 'unfiltered Fringe.' Over the years, it's been a difficult struggle to have these two very different platforms contained under one umbrella. For the ultimate self-actualization of our goals, there needs to be a fundamental clarity about what's the hell's going on." Organizational efforts are underway in order to draw more of a distinction between the two platforms. "As we sort of evolved away from the concept of 'fringe'—which is high-volume, low-context, and not a sort of reasoned body of programming—we had this process. We called it 'the net': We cast a big net, an open call for work. Whatever work landed in 'the net,' we were then obligated to choose from," Stucchio explains. That system is now being further refined: "We want to change that process. We're doing so this year, we're abandoning 'the net' and we're going with fishing lines. We're targeting what kind of work we're looking for. We like to look for work that is pushing the boundary of a form in some way. We see so much work—locally, I know exactly what's happening as much as I can. So we know what the baseline is. Occasionally, those folks who are deftly moving something in an interesting direction . . . that's interesting and exciting. All of the presenters I know around the country are all looking for the same thing—that new voice, that fresh approach for something."

Payments/Profits/Benefits: A past payment sampling: Artists performing on a full bill get about 60 percent of their box office; those on a double bill get about 35 percent; and triple-billers get 25 percent. Performers appearing in free shows will be paid a fee as well. In terms of helping artists network, the fest pays train/airfare/hotel accommodations for some scouting producers.

Physical Production Details: The majority of shows are multiple bills and are presented in multi-use venues that have standard light and sound. A venue manager at each space will help with tech needs. The Fringe will help participants hunt down site-specific spaces (ask early) or outdoor spaces. There's a late night cabaret space as well.

Housing: Inquire about availability/arrangements if chosen.

Past Artists/Productions of Note: Sarah Jones.

Festival Flavor: There's a strong stripe of local pride running through this fest. "One of our fundamental values here is a belief and a position in local art," says Stucchio. "Local performers—it's the backbone, it's the reason we've had the success we've had. There's a lot of really incredible, strong work happening in Philly in that world of experimental performance. New Paradise Laboratories, Pig Iron Theatre Company, Headlong Dance Theatre—really smart, smart work, and there's a lot of other stuff. So we're ridin' the backs of this work—it's the basis of a lot of our work now, in the past, and in the future. As it gets better, we're gonna get better."

The Bottom Line: Stucchio and his associates are warm and supportive folks who really care about great art and great artists. A terrific place to work.

Prague Fringe Festival, Czech Republic

Founded: 2000

Contact Info: The best way to get in touch with this fest is through e-mail at info@praguefringe.com

Web site: *www.praguefringe.com*

Performance Dates: Annually for about five days in June.

The Festival's Mission: Founder and artistic director Steven Gove is a native of Scotland and was longtime manager at the Assembly Theatre in Edinburgh, one of the Edinburgh Fringe's biggest venues. His impetus for starting this fringe began as follows: "I moved to the Czech Republic in 1997 just for the chance of an overseas experience, and really at that time had no intention of living here. Very quickly, I sort of fell in love with the place. I was teaching English initially, and every year I was going back to Edinburgh to attend the Fringe there. I got to the point where I was done teaching English, and wanted to get back into theater. So three of us sat down at a table at the festival in Edinburgh one particular year and said, Why don't we do a fringe festival in Prague? From those first moments, we basically came into existence." His co-founders were Carole Wears, a theater manager in Newcastle, and Angus Coull, a media professional who'd worked extensively through Scotland.

Application Specifics: "We started to spread the word with people we knew (at Edinburgh)," explains Gove in regard to how he attracted artists for the first Prague Fringe. "The following year, which was 2001, we went armed with lots of lovely new business cards and specifically went out looking for new shows, to try and get some interest going. It was actually quite amazing, because right from the first moment, people somehow believed that the Prague Fringe had been going for a number of years already. 'Oh, the Prague Fringe . . . oh, yeah!' It was actually quite funny. In the second year, we put together an application, and we made a point on the Web site that, this is an open festival, and people can apply to come in." See Web site for latest guidelines; there is some curation in regard to programming self-presenting (i.e., uninvited) companies.

Fees: There's a nominal participation fee (see Web site for latest requirement). In some cases, fees can be waived.

Selection Criteria: "I think when we sit down to look at the performances, one of the things we look at is suitability of the performance in Prague," explains Gove. "It's not an English-speaking country, although English is the second language here, and English is spoken very strongly. Something that might throw us off would be a very heavily text-based show, which would not be accessible to the local audience here. It could also be something like, just perhaps a show where there's no relevance to what's going on here at all. I think some of the shows that we've received applications from have obviously been shows that have been successful—the companies have sent really interesting packs, and wonderful reviews—but just the sense that people here would not get it. Particularly, if shows are visual, it's obviously easier to transfer a show over to somewhere like Prague." Shows also might not get accepted due to a lack of a feasible space to stage the show in, or if they're too technically demanding.

Payments/Profits/Benefits: A 60 percent door split.

Physical Production Details: "Each company will have a fixed get-in time and minimal rehearsal time," says Gove of teching within venues, which are Prague theatres. "It's quite tight. It's very like Edinburgh, in the sense that there's maybe five, six, seven companies that are gonna be in the one space, and shows are starting from like four o'clock. And obviously, we don't have the theatres for a week before—it's like two days before, or in some cases, a day before. So it's very, very tight turnaround and there is limited rehearsal time, definitely." Tech is included within the rehearsal time; each company has fifty minutes to get in and fifty minutes to strike.

Housing: Inquire about arranging accommodations. In recent years, festival participants who have been invited to the fringe have received a free full stay. Self-presenting companies must pay their own expenses.

Past Artists/Productions of Note: The Canadian show *Tuesdays & Sundays*, which enjoyed a sold-out run; productions by the UK groups Wishbone and Lulu's Living Room.

Festival Flavor: Gove tries to be as accommodating and considerate of artists as possible. For instance, he offers letters to groups stating they've been accepted to the Fringe so that they can seek funding, quite a nice rarity among fests.

The Bottom Line: The Czech Republic's popularity with young Americans ensures strong networking possibilities, not to mention a great cultural experience at this very high-quality fringe.

San Francisco Fringe Festival

Founded: 1991

Contact Info: San Francisco Fringe Festival, EXIT Theatre, 156 Eddy Street, San Francisco, CA 94102
(415) 931-1033 (phone); (415) 931-2699 (fax)
E-mail: mail@sffringe.org
Web site: *www.sffringe.org*

Performance Dates: Annually for approximately ten days in September.

The Festival's Mission: It's totally unjuried and unfettered artistically. This fest splits its performances into two categories: standard venue (in which shows are assigned space and limited to an hour of showtime) and Bring Your Own Venue (in which show personnel hunt down their own space, and can perform within it as long as they like).

Application Specifics: The most current application form will be available at the Fringe's Web site. Potential fringers from northern California are picked through a lottery system; all others are taken first-come, first-served.

Fees: For standard venue shows, $475 per company/individual; for Bring Your Own Venue, $350 per company/individual. A non-refundable $25 fee is also charged to everyone.

Selection Criteria: None.

Payments/Profits/Benefits: 100 percent of the box office returns to each company. The Fringe has a Frequent Fringer admission pass system as well; $5 from each pass used is given to each company.

Physical Production Details: An SM per show must be provided by each company/individual in order to get your show taken seriously by production manager Jason Ries. Each show is provided a Fringe techie, and each show gets to tech free for two and a half hours (more time can possibly be arranged for $20 per hour). Scripts must be cue-marked for the techie to be able to tech/run your show. Minimal props are available, but there are two pianos. No storage space available. Pyro must be negotiated in advance.

Past Artists/Productions of Note: *Disco Prophecies; Demon Pope; Corned Beef.*

Festival Flavor: A good-natured, helpful staff makes this fringe a great place to work.

The Bottom Line: A must-have experience!

Toronto Fringe Festival, Canada

Founded: 1989

Contact Info: The Toronto Fringe Theatre Festival, 344 Floor Street West, Suite 507, Toronto, ON M5S 3A7 Canada

(416) 966-1062 (phone); (416) 966-5072 (fax)

E-mail: fringe@fringetoronto.com

Web site: *www.fringetoronto.com*

Performance Dates: Annually each June-July, for approximately twelve days.

The Festival's Mission: The Toronto Fringe is in many ways a godchild of the Edmonton Fringe. Inspired by Edmonton's trailblazing audacity and booming audience numbers, the Toronto Fringe followed its free-for-all model and started off presenting a modest forty productions in four venues—always with a view toward offering artists maximum support and creative leeway.

Application Specifics: Request an application by mail or fax, or visit Web site at above address. There are three slot categories: 60-minute max performance time, 90-minute max performance time, or KidsVenue slots (for children's productions).

Fees: An application fee of approximately $600.

Selection Criteria: A lottery is used to choose. Also, there's a quota system: 75 percent of accepted companies are from Ontario, 15 percent are Canadian, and 10 percent are international.

Payments/Profits/Benefits: A seven-performance guarantee (or eight if you get a KidsVenue slot) and 100 percent of box office profits. Published plays that have premiered at the Fringe are also sold through the festival's online play library.

Physical Production Details: Venues vary depending upon show. Each company/artist is assigned a technician for show run.

Housing: Not provided, but the Fringe will try to help you network your way to free local lodging.

Past Artists/Productions of Note: Tons of eclectic offerings, including Sky Gilbert's *Drag Queens in Outer Space*, *Bash* by Tony Berto, *Frida K* by Gloria Montero, and *Top Gun! The Musical* by Dennis McGrath.

Festival Flavor: "Toronto is kind of the New York of Canada for theater," says TJ Dawe. "All of the venues are real theaters, rather than things that have been turned into theaters, but they're also really far apart, so you have to drive or take transit."

The Bottom Line: If you're Canadian, a must. If you're from elsewhere, give this fest a shot—if you make it past the quota limit, you'll find yourself performing in an incredibly vibrant environment.

Vancouver Fringe Festival

Founded: 1984

Contact Info: Kirsten Schrader, Acting Executive Artistic Director, Vancouver Fringe Festival, 1402 Anderson Street, Vancouver, BC V6H 3R6 Canada

(604) 257-0350 (phone); (604) 253-1924 (fax)

E-mail: associateproducer@vancouverfringe.com

Web site: *www.vancouverfringe.com*

Performances Dates: Annually for eleven days in September.

The Festival's Mission: "Theatre for everyone." The Fringe's acting executive artistic director, Kirsten Schrader, strives to serve the needs of audience members of all ages. To this end, she explains, "One of the things I started in 2003 is KidsFringe, because our mandate is 'theatre for everyone,' but we had nothing for kids. KidsFringe has two components: one is KidsVenue, which is ticketed theater shows for kids; and Family Days, and on the fringe weekends, during the festival, it's free outdoor performance for kids—storytelling, stilt-walkers, plays, and music."

Application Specifics: Applications are accepted in the following order of preference: in person; online; by fax; by mail.

See Web site at above address to study the various types of applications to choose the one that's right for your work.

Fees: Inquire about current requirements.

Selection Criteria: Unjuried; children's programming, however, is screened for appropriateness of content.

Payments/Profits/Benefits: "We're different from other Fringes in that performers get paid on a three-payout schedule," says Schrader. "So on this date they get paid, on this date they get paid, and on this date they get paid, whereas other festivals will pay them out that night, or pay them out the next day." Inquire about current payment scale. Schrader also notes that many casting directors and scouts scour this fringe for talent: "The payoffs can be huge."

Physical Production Details: Nine standard spaces, which range from theaters to galleries; eleven Bring Your Own Venue sites, which range from churches to bars to theaters to galleries to parking garages. "We don't provide rehearsal space, so performers have to rehearse somewhere else," says Schrader. "There's a tech rehearsal. If they're in town, we take them on a tour of the venue, and they talk about whatever they need to talk about with our production manager, who's very experienced and has a really great team. Then there's a tech rehearsal, and then the show starts. In terms of being in the actual space before the show starts, it varies. Some people go in much earlier, up to maybe an hour earlier and start warming up or whatever they do, and some people arrive a half-hour before and just sort of start."

Housing: Not provided.

Past Artists/Productions of Note: Schrader recalls, "We had one woman, Meghan Gardner, this past year who was straight out of an acting school here. She did a show called *Dissolve* about Rohypnol, the date-rape drug. There was a rash of date-rape drug incidents in the city this past summer, so it was very timely. She did it so cleverly; she was the drug itself, and she was selling herself in the show, so she was saying, you know, 'I can make you feel so wonderful, I can make you lose all your inhibitions!' So there was a different twist on it, and she got so much media coverage, she sold out a lot of shows. It was great—she was straight out of school, and she's creating a name for herself now, and she's gotten tons of roles from it."

Festival Flavor: "We really are looking at reducing our deficit, and we feel, we want to become the most professional fringe, in that our efficiency, our systems, we test them," explains Schrader. "We want to be of service in the best way, and be the most efficient we can be."

The Bottom Line: Schrader's goals, in tandem with her board of directors, include making this fringe "the best-attended, best-run, and best example of the fringe concept in Canada." These folks know what they're doing, so climb aboard.

Victoria Fringe Festival/Uno Festival of Solo Performance, Canada

Founded: 1987, Fringe; 1997, Uno

Contact Info: Janet Munsil, Producer, Intrepid Theatre, 3rd Floor—1014 Government Street, Victoria, BC V8W 1X7 Canada
(250) 383-2663 (phone); (250) 380-1999 (fax)

E-mail: info@intrepidtheatre.com

Web site: *www.intrepidtheatre.com*

Performance Dates: Fringe, annually in August-September; Uno Fest, annually in May.

The Festivals' Missions: Victoria may be one of the smallest open Fringes in Canada, but it is certainly large in artistic value. Janet Munsil, its producer, "We're a small organization—there's only two people here year-round—and we're very hands-on. I think when you get into larger organizations, it's harder sometimes. When the festival's larger, there's so many people to keep track of. We stay small." As for Uno, which endeavors to give strong solo performers a showcase and outlet, it evolved out of another fest Munsil oversaw. "We'd been doing a multi-disciplinary women's festival that had film, music, theater, and visual art," says Munsil. "We found that we were experiencing a bit of backlash from women who thought that the festival was too political and weren't coming. Another group of women thought the festival wasn't political enough. Really, we were just trying to showcase artists; politics were far from our minds. So we thought, if nobody wants this festival, let's stop doing it, which was too bad, so we were looking around for another kind of festival to do. When we looked at what had been popular at the Fringe festival, and really where a lot of the most exciting work that we had seen was happening, it was with solo performance, performer-written work."

Application Specifics: Contact Intrepid for latest guidelines/application forms, and/or check Web site at above address.

Fees: The Fringe requires $454.75 to participate, plus a $25 application fee. Uno charges a $30 application fee. For Uno, submit a videotape and/or script, press clippings, reviews, and your resume.

Selection Criteria: The Fringe is unjuried; the Uno Fest is juried. Ten Uno selections are programmed to get three performances apiece.

Payments/Profits/Benefits: If you're a Fringer, you get 100 percent of your box office. For Uno artists, fees are negotiated. Uno artists receive a fee plus travel expenses.

Physical Production Details: "We have four regular Fringe venues which are each programmed in rep, with usually eight companies," says Munsil. "People do arrive in town at various times at the week the Fringe gets rolling. Because we sometimes overlap with either the Edmonton or Vancouver festivals, sometimes we have to do technical rehearsals for people mid-Fringe, or right before their first show. But generally they get two or three hours of technical rehearsal in the space with their technician, which we provide. There's not a lot of lighting and sound equipment—it's a very basic sort of set-up. They usually get a couple of specials. Many of the shows that happen in the Fringe, either the companies have been touring the whole country so they can come in and get it set up in thirty minutes, or it's the first time they've produced it a full-length play with thirty people in it! It runs the whole gamut of experiences." If you haven't had a lot of stage tech experience, don't worry— Jan and her people will try their best to help you out. Uno is presented at the Belfry Arts Center in either a 280-seat house or a 90-seat house with CD player, MiniDisc, mic, and projection capabilities. A three-hour tech with techie provided. Site-specific spaces can also be negotiated.

Housing: It's here, and it's free for everyone. Fringe associates, even Fringe audience members, are happy to put artists up. Uno artists are guaranteed accommodations.

Past Artists/Productions of Note: TJ Dawe and Shannan Calcutt, to name a couple luminaries.

Festival Flavors: "*The Craig* is our audience review publication," says Munsil. "We do a print version and an online version, and the audience submits their reviews of the shows. We don't edit it, we don't check their spelling. The audience feedback is really important. It's such a big part of the Fringe, because performers and the audience are all right in that soup together. They're standing in line for the shows, people recognize each other. Everyone who comes to our Fringe has a little button that they wear, so you can tell who's at the Fringe. So I think the community aspect of it is really important." The Uno Fest consists primarily of previously, recently produced work. "It's more of a soft-seat theater audience," says Munsil.

The Bottom Line: Jan Munsil is a lovely person to deal with—
being an artist herself, she understands and respects other
artists' needs. Definitely work with these fests if you can.

Wellington Fringe Festival, New Zealand

Founded: 1993

Contact Info: Timi Renner, Director, Fringe NZ Office, Level 1,
58–60 Victoria Street, P.O. Box 6596, Wellington New Zealand
(64) 4 495-8015 (phone); (64) 4 495-8015 (fax)

E-mail: tim@fringe.org.nz

Web site: *www.fringe.org.nz*

Performance Dates: Annually for about one month each February
-March.

The Festival's Mission: To be as radical as possible in its artistic
offerings. Innovative, controversial, and daring theater works
abound here.

Application Specifics: This fringe's registration specifics vary from
year to year, so contact the administrative office at the above
address for the latest guidelines.

Fees: Inquire about latest requirements. There's one flat registration fee, as a rule.

Selection Criteria: You can literally do anything here, and there's
no cap on the number of participants, or limits on performers' countries of origin.

Payments/Profits/Benefits: Inquire about latest guidelines.

Physical Production Details: Wildly varied all over Wellington.
Inquire about latest venues/tech specifics.

Housing: Not provided.

Past Artists/Productions of Note: *Mr. Fungus; Ultra Super Vixen
Women with Really Enormous Tits, The Three Canadians
Attempt Ben Hur; Puppet Ninja.*

Festival Flavor: If you're getting the drift that this fringe is glori-
ously out there, you're right. This fest expects you not to need

your hand held; if you're coming to New Zealand from out of the country, you must be diligent in terms of planning. You have to do a lot of legwork on your own terms of securing up-to-date information, but the creative payoffs are limitless.

A few highlights: In addition to the risky live stagework presented, the fest kicks off with a Drag Race (cross-dressing participants literally dash down a main Wellington street) and offers great networking opportunities (check out the Fringe Café section of the fest's Web site, where paying jobs actually get posted!).

The Bottom Line: One of the world's best fringes for unbridled, shocking, beautiful art. If you go, make the most of the experience. See as many shows as you can, and try to hook up with like-minded potential collaborators.

Winnipeg Fringe Festival, Canada

Founded: 1987

Contact Info: 174 Market Street, Winnipeg, MB
R3B 0P8 Canada
(204) 956-1340 (phone)

E-mail: fringe@mtc.mb.ca

Web site: *www.winnipegfringe.com*

Performance Dates: Annually for twelve days each July.

The Festival's Mission: Another descendent of the Edmonton Fringe in philosophy. The Winnipeg Fringe's primary goal was, and is, to facilitate cutting edge theater companies in bringing their work to the local community, spotlighting both fresh international work and new local performers.

Application Specifics: Check Web site at above address for current specifics.

Fees: Check Web site at above address for current specifics.

Selection Criteria: There is a quota system to sift through local, national, and individual applicants that varies yearly in terms, plus a lottery; other than that, it's first-come, first-served.

Payments/Profits/Benefits: 100 percent of ticket revenue goes back to performing companies, with the exception of an advance-sale surcharge to cover some limited costs for the Fringe.

Physical Production Details: The Fringe's twenty-two venues are all centrally located around Winnipeg's Old Market Square, and it's just a five-minute stroll from venue to venue. Spaces range from a planetarium to a traditional playhouse and outdoor stages.

Housing: Inquire about availability.

Past Artists/Productions of Note: TJ Dawe.

Festival Flavor: "Winnipeg is a tremendous festival—front page of the newspaper," says TJ Dawe. "It's a really big festival town, and their cultural life is huge. And people often brag to me: It's the coldest densely populated city in the world—colder than Moscow, colder than Helsinki, anything you could name."

The Bottom Line: Very worthwhile for Canadians companies looking to make a splash.

Section 2

Performance-Driven Festivals

BAM Next Wave Festival (Brooklyn Academy of Music)

Founded: 1981, unofficially; 1983, officially

Contact Info: Joseph V. Melillo, Executive Producer,
   Brooklyn Academy of Music, 30 Lafayette Avenue,
   Brooklyn, NY 11217
   (718) 636-4100 (phone)

E-mail: programming@bam.org

Web site: *www.bam.org*

Performance Dates: A three-month series of performances
   every fall.

The Festival's Mission: Melillo stresses that the Next Wave
   Festival's intent is "to present contemporary non-traditional
   work from the global performing arts community in all
   genres." The festival offers intensely innovative theater, dance,
   musical, and opera works, helping to introduce audiences to
   acclaimed artists including Robert Wilson, Laurie Anderson,
   Phillip Glass, Bill T. Jones, Mark Morris, and many, many

others. The work of Anne Bogart, Peter Brook, and many internationally distinguished companies also grace the festival, which also devotes a festival season to exploring the culture of a single country (such as Australia, spotlighted during the wildly successful 2001 Next Wave Down Under).

FYI: Only fully staged, previously produced productions are eligible for the Next Wave; a videotape of your performers, plus any promo materials you feel might be helpful, should be sent to the address above. BAM staff members also try to attend live performances of productions when possible.

Application Specifics: Obviously, BAM is highly selective in regard to Next Wave Festival programming. Although renowned artists have a strong presence (as do companies and artists whose work is well regarded by festival personnel), BAM will consider unsolicited material.

Fees: Not applicable.

Selection Criteria: "Compelling artistic merit of the work; productions values; clarity of the storytelling," says Melillo.

Payment/Profits/Benefits: Artist arrangements are individual and confidential. Prestige factor is incomparable; there are few greater creative honors than to perform live in this forum.

Physical Production Details: The Howard Gilman Opera House (a majestic 2,109 seat house) and the Harvey Theater (874 seats). Pieces have also been presented in smaller venues, like the 300-seat Leperq Space.

Housing: Only artists selected to present should inquire about policy.

Past Artists/Productions of Note: Melillo cites the following as particular creative milestones: "Robert Wilson's collaborations with composer/musician Tom Waits and Lou Reed." He adds, "The music theater form has had a consistent place within the Next Wave Festival, and that will continue into the future."

The Bottom Line: For established professionals, the crème de la crème. For most emerging artists, something to strive for—keep the festival abreast of your highest-quality work.

Belfast Festival, Ireland

Founded: 1962

Contact Info: Belfast Festival, 25 College Gardens, Belfast BT9 6BS Ireland.

+44 (0) 28 9027 2600 (phone)

Web site: *www.belfastfestival.com*

Performances Dates: Annually for about two weeks in October-November.

The Festival's Mission: The biggest arts festival in Ireland endeavors to present great international artists working in theater, dance, music, literature, visual arts, and comedy. In the words of the festival's esteemed director, Stella Hall, "My view would be that now, the role of a festival is not simply to reflect artists back at themselves, but to provide opportunities to engage with international artists on a level playing field and on an equal basis. What is available in Belfast and Northern Ireland year-round is a constant, steady stream of Irish artists talking about themselves. I think therefore that the festival must provide alternative voices, particularly at this moment, addressing the issue of cultural diversity, the issue of diverse communities, and the issue of Ireland as a place to which migrations occur, rather than a place from which migration takes place. We should be welcoming in the Chinese, the Indian, the Eastern European. Unless we have strong, positive cultural images of those cultures, we will disrespect and downgrade them."

Application Specifics: Send a written proposal about what you'd like to do to the address above, and wait to be contacted.

Fees: Not applicable.

Selection Criteria: "In terms of the choices that I make, it's under the program I present," explains Hall. "There has to be a balance of work that is made here, which reflects local concerns, and work that is made elsewhere that reflects other cultural priorities. In terms of work that's made here, I would be looking for work that takes the artist onto a level plane. Either it challenges the form, or it's on a bigger scale, or it engages with different concerns than they would normally engage with. If they are also able to address something that celebrates the creativity of the city in a way that will engage audiences from further afield, then I'm even more positive, because I want work to travel from here. Quite a bit of the work is so locally specific that it doesn't travel."

Payments/Profits/Benefits: Inquire if selected. Needless to say, the exposure is priceless. Additionally, Hall wishes to help good work reach as many people as possible. "I invest in productions," she explains. "Then it's up to the companies themselves to tour." What kind of work travels best, in her opinion? "Although I say that I want work to travel, it doesn't necessarily have to travel physically. It can travel in people's minds, or it can travel by reputation."

Physical Production Details: Forty-one venues in the vicinity of Queen's university, ranging from theater spaces to halls to churches to bars and cafés.

Housing: Inquire about availability if accepted.

Past Artists/Productions of Note: Everything from the Royal Shakespeare Company to Jimi Hendrix to Lawrence Olivier to Dizzy Gillespie to Michael Palin of *Monty Python* fame.

Festival Flavor: Hall reflects upon two rule-breaking theater pieces from the respected Irish company Tinderbox: "One very positive one is *Northern Star*, which Tinderbox produced at such a high level of competence it should have toured internationally. It didn't really have the infrastructure to make that possible. Tinderbox commissioned six Northern Irish writers to create short pieces of work to be performed only in the very specific site of Crumlin Road Courthouse, which is of course resonant with history. That was an event that couldn't travel out physically because of the very specific location of it, but could travel out through recording, through broadcast." Hall cites this production's fine writing, production values, and staging, and "iconoclastic approach to theater-making that they took in making that piece of work."

The Bottom Line: Hall is working toward the future goal of commissioning international work that speaks to Belfast and setting up artist residencies. The bar is set high, but keep this fest abreast of your work, and if you get the chance to work here, jump at it.

Caracas International Theatre Festival, Venezuela

Founded: 1973

Contact Info: Carmen Ramia, general director, Caracas International Theatre Festival, Edif Rajatabla, Plaza Morelos, Los Caobos, Venezuela
2-571-42-19, 2-571-91-57 (phone numbers)

Web site: *www.fitcaracas.com*

Performance Dates: Bi-annually for two weeks in March-April.

The Festival's Mission: Widely considered to be the top festival in all of Latin America, the "Festival International de Teatro Caracas" (nicknamed FITC) pioneered the concept of bringing together noteworthy international performing artists in this region, which is still its major goal today. Regional outreach is also a major intention; companies from various points in Venezuela are invited to present their work as well.

Applications Specifics: Recent fests average about sixteen participating companies, from Latin America, the

United States, Asia, and Europe. Proposals are made and accepted from various organizations; the catch is, you must be well-known and/or well-regarded. Still, it pays to introduce yourself by inquiring about proposal specifics, because FITC is also known to embrace the unusual and unexpected, especially if it comes in the form of highly skilled multidisciplinary work.

Fees: Not applicable.

Selection Criteria: Material genres range from trade productions to wildly avant-garde stuff. This festival is appropriately choosy when it comes to international artists, as it endeavors to introduce very strong international work to local audiences. A big part of the festival, though, is also to act as a springboard for promising young Venezuelan performers. If you get your work into the lineup here, expect to be scouted by many producers from other fests in Latin America and Europe.

Payments/Profits/Benefits: Inquire if selected.

Physical Production Details: Theater spaces include the Sala Rios Reyna, the Sala Juan Bautista at the National Library Plaza, the Sala Anna Julia Rojas at the Ateneo de Caracas, the Celarge, and many more. Street theater is also a huge component, many groups also perform in open spaces throughout Caracas.

Housing: Inquire about availability if selected.

Past Artists/Productions of Note: Peter Brook; Joseph Chaiken; Els Juglars, a popular Spanish theater troupe; *I Bought a Shovel to Dig My Own Grave*, presented by Carniceria Teatro; *I'm a Fool to Want You*, presented by the UK company Told By An Idiot.

Festival Flavor: Political unrest caused the delay of the fest for several weeks in 2004, as demonstrations and violence turned the streets of Caracas quite chaotic. One of the most wonderful and admirable traits of this fest is its ability to persevere, however—only two companies ended up withdrawing from the highly successful final program. There is a definite "can-do" spunk that permeates the atmosphere at this fest; no matter what language the artist next to you may be speaking, changes are you'll both have resolve and determination in common if you've made the cut here, both creatively and personally.

The Bottom Line: If you're an artist of high caliber, absolutely give this one a go—you'll find lots of support from fest personnel and a great sense of camaraderie from fellow artists. Stay safe, though.

Dublin Theatre Festival

Founded: 1957

Contact Info: Dublin Theatre Festival, 44 East Essex Street, Temple Bar, Dublin 2 Ireland

+353 1 677 8439 (phone); +353 1 679 7709 (fax)

E-mail: info@dublintheatrefestival.com

Web site: *www.dublintheatrefestival.com*

Performance Dates: Annually in October.

The Festival's Mission: This festival largely explores the many facets of modern Irish theater and society—but its intent encompasses excellent work from many different sensibilities as well. Festival Director Fergus Linehan says, "You try to do work that isn't terribly localized. I think there's productions that are put on that are effectively for the local community, and don't have any aspirations beyond that. What you'd hope to do is use the sort of slightly rarefied atmosphere of the festival to allow people to maybe kind of broaden their horizons a little bit. We sort of use this word that isn't a word—the 'internalization' of theatre, where an Irish project has aspirations or is dealing with something or drawing on either people to physically come in and work on it, or influences which are from outside of Ireland. Anything that kind of builds bridges from Ireland into other cultures—there would be a general preference toward that."

Application Specifics: Primarily Irish artists are showcased—half the program is devoted typically to original Irish works and some revivals. Contact the theater to request current submission guidelines.

Fees: Not applicable.

Selection Criteria: "There are some practical considerations," says Linehan. "There are a certain amount of parameters within which you work, and your personal preferences operate within that. On the one hand, you've got your audience, who have an enormous say in what you do, so you've got a basic knowledge of the audience here in Dublin and the festival audience, and how far you can push them. You can maybe have one, perhaps two, foreign language pieces in any given year. There's obviously going to be more sympathy toward recognizable companies like maybe Steppenwolf in the U.S., or certain writers or certain novelists. Because we work in fairly large venues, the issue of recognition is given a lot of consideration. The weight of the festival will give you a certain number of cards you can play in terms of no familiarity at all. But once you've gone beyond that, you do need some connection with the audience, and that connection might be as simple as, it's a production of *Hamlet*, or it's a David Mamet play that people might know, or something like that. You're looking for an Irish connection, maybe, where it's sort of an interpretation of something that might be conventionally Irish, but the interpretation is something that's kind of fresh to us—someone else looking at something through new eyes."

Payments/Profits/Benefits: Inquire if selected.

Physical Production Details: The Abbey Theatre; the Gaiety Theatre; the Gate Theatre; the Liberty Hall Theatre; the

O'Reilly Theatre; the Olympia Theatre; the Peacock Theatre; the Samuel Beckett Theatre; the Ark; and the Tivoli Theatre. Venues range from approximately 300 to 500 seats.

Housing: Inquire about availability if selected.

Past Artists/Productions of Note: *Woyzeck*, directed by Robert Wilson, with music by Tom Waits; work by Peter Brook; work by Neil Armfield of Australia's Company B; many, many more extraordinary artists of the highest standard.

Festival Flavor: The fest has a decidedly political bent, holding symposiums on Irish societal issues as well as extensive analysis of and debate about theater criticism. Linehan notes as well: "Irish theatre can be very, very 'kitchen sink-y.' In an ideal world, you would hope that you're trying to provoke work that's maybe a little bit more urban and a little bit more eclectic, a little more cosmopolitan."

The Bottom Line: The perfect forum for smart, internationally versed artists to express themselves in.

Edge of the World Theater Festival (EdgeFest)

Founded: circa early 2000s

Contact Info: EdgeFest, P.O. Box 931301, Los Angeles, CA 90093-1301
(310) 281-7920 (phone)

E-mail: info@edgeoftheworld.org

Web site: *www.edgeoftheworld.org*

Performance Dates: Annually three weekends and six days in October.

The Festival's Mission: Officially: "To contribute to the evolution of theater in Los Angeles, to broaden and strengthen the audience for our work, and to inspire Los Angeles theater artists to create innovative and exciting pieces that are unique to the theatrical experience and push the boundaries of what is possible. To do this, EdgeFest offers a curated

showcase of around fifty L.A.-area experimental theater
productions.

Application Specifics: Los Angeles–based companies only
may apply (out-of-towners may participate only if hosted
or co-produced by a local group). Productions must have had
twelve performances or less to be eligible. Submit a short
synopsis of the production you want to do, a script or video
sample of your work, the names of all collaborators on your
production, and any available reviews. See Web site for most
up-to-date additional application specifics.

Fees: A $75 application fee (non-refundable).

Selection Criteria: All projects chosen for inclusion will be of
high artistic merit, will fit appropriately within EdgeFest's
creative philosophy, and will be innovative in terms of
material/interpretation.

Payments/Profits/Benefits: It's all up to you, as each selected
company is required to locate its own performance venue and
negotiate all contract terms with that venue. EdgeFest can
help you get a good deal (like a generous box-office split
with a venue, or a discount rental arrangement), but ask early
for help.

Physical Production Details: Some EdgeFest-friendly venues are
clustered near each other, primarily in Hollywood, to make
it easier for audience members to take in as many shows
as possible.

Housing: Not applicable.

Past Artists/Productions of Note: *Dorothy—After Oz* by Ginna
Carter; *No Justice, No Peace* by Hermosa Beach Players.

Festival Flavor: You definitely have to be able to work
independently to thrive at EdgeFest. The festival will
promote your work through its print program and Web
site, but you must be responsible for all of your own business concerns, as well as focused on putting your best foot
forward creatively. The atmosphere is ripe for networking:

Symposiums, discussions, and feedback sessions abound here, so don't be shy.

The Bottom Line: The EdgeFest moniker is a strong endorsement for your work—take advantage of it.

Festival of Autumn (Festival D'Automne), France

Founded: 1999

Contact Info: Festival of Autumn in Paris, 156 Street of Rivoli, 75001 Paris, France

0153451700 (phone); 0153451701 (fax)

E-mail: info@festival-automne.com

Web site: *www.festival-automne.com*

Performance Dates: Annually for about one week in September-October.

The Festival's Mission: To fuse a variety of forms of contemporary art—theater, dance, music, and visual arts—against the very cosmopolitan backdrop of Paris. Festival director Alaín Crombeque has set forth a very avant-garde artistic agenda as well, programming multi-lingual work that doesn't shy away from controversial political or economic issues.

Application Specifics: This festival is heavily, heavily selective, platforming some of the world's most prestigious artists and companies. Contact the fest to inquire about sending a sample of your work to be considered ONLY if you are extremely serious and accomplished.

Fees: Not applicable.

Selection Criteria: A very strong mix of international work is among this festival's trademarks. Routinely, performers from New York, China, Iran, South Africa, and France itself intermingle within the confines of the festival. Eclecticism rules here in terms of how festival offerings are balanced yearly.

Payments/Profits/Benefits: Confidential. Inquire if selected.

Physical Production Details: Lush, gorgeous spaces such as
the Theatre of the Bastille, the Odeon, the House of Creteil
Arts, Theatre of the City, and the Theatre Nanterre-Almond
Trees. Tech specifics dictated by the festival within these
spaces.

Housing: Inquire about availability if selected.

Past Artists/Productions of Note: Laurie Anderson, Nan Goldin,
Jenny Holzer, DJ Spooky, Simon McBurney, Haruki
Murakami.

Festival Flavor: Although a lot of the work presented at this fest
is intense in its social commentary, puppet theater has played
a surprisingly significant role here as well. The Duke Quartet
and Handspring Puppet Company collaborated with South
African artists William Kentridge and Kevin Yolans on a
memorable 2001 puppet operetta. The Italian troupe Societas
Raffaello Sanzio also reinterpreted "Tom Thumb" to great
acclaim that year.

The Bottom Line: If you can get to Europe, soak up this fest in
person before you ever dare attempt to approach it as an
artist. Just immersing yourself in the spectacle as an audience
member is a once-in-a-lifetime experience. If after viewing
work here you think your stuff is simpatico, be sure your
material is flawless before making a proposal.

Göteborg Dance and Theatre Festival, Sweden

Founded: 1994

Contact Info: Brigitta Winnberg-Rydh, Artistic Director,
Göteborg Dance and Theatre Festival, Jamtorgsgatan 12,
SE-413 01, Göteborg, Sweden
+46 (0) 31-711 65 93 (fax)

E-mail: festival@kultur.goteborg.se

Web site: *www.festival.goteborg.se*

Performance Dates: Biennially in August for about a week.

The Festival's Mission: To expose the local arts community and citizenship to the best international performing arts pieces possible. This fest is considered tops in quality in all of Sweden. Primarily non-English-speaking audiences, needless to say, but work is presented in every language imaginable.

Application Specifics: Juried. Contact the festival to find out current proposal requirements. A well-organized workshop and seminar program offers additional educational and professional opportunities to invited artists, as well as other interested visiting performers and fest-goers.

Fees: Inquire about current guidelines for workshop and seminar participation.

Selection Criteria: The Cultural Department of Göteborg, as the fest's governing body, seeks out work it deems "interesting," and traditionally chooses a central theme for each fest.
In the past, themes have included, for example, innovations in circus art. There is a very healthy range of variation on subject matter weaving through and around the outskirts of the fest, however, with children's programming, rock-and-roll performance art, monologue pieces—the kitchen sink, really.

Payments/Profits/Benefits: Inquire about current guidelines if selected, but know in advance that many performers here work for free. A major bonus, though: This fest is a networking goldmine. Producers, directors, and film distributors from all over the world flood the fest, cherry-picking the talent.

Physical Production Details: Many performances are held in the company's organization headquarters, which includes a very nice performance space. Other performances take place around the area, including a rose garden, the nightclub (Klubb Trampolin), and the Göteborg Opera.

Housing: Not generally provided, but the fest is very generous in terms of offering suggestions for affordable lodging.

Past Artists/Productions of Note: *Alive from Palestine—Stories Under Occupation; The Spheres; Three Dark Tales.*

Festival Flavor: Very melting-pot in scope. West Swedish theater companies often collaborate with Egyptian theater artists, and numerous festival offerings melding these two cultures have played to great reception. Tango performances have been popular in the past; so have cowboy-themed performances from the UK. Anything goes.

The Bottom Line: An extremely well-organized and professional gathering that offers an incredible opportunity to introduce your work to crowds who've never seen anything like it before. Plus, you can make connections for days.

The Holland Festival, Amsterdam

Founded: 1947

Contact Info: Attn: Maaike van Gejin/research, Holland Festival, Kleine-Gartmanpantsoen 21 1017 RP, Amsterdam, The Netherlands
0031 (0) 20-5307110 (phone)

E-mail: info@hollandfestival.nl

Web site: *www.hollandfstvl.nl*

Performance Dates: Annually for about three weeks in June.

The Festival's Mission: To encourage artists in Holland and worldwide to make radical dramatic statements while still keeping theatrical traditions in mind.

Applications Specifics: Submit a proposal package to Maaike van Geijn at the above address. Include a full project proposal/outline, applicable reviews, and a CD or videotape with a "live" bio on it in lieu of a traditional resume. DO NOT SUBMIT THE FOLLOWING: folklore-based music, dance, or theatre; puppet theatre, circus, or street performance; classical recitals or reprises; overseas orchestra pieces; Middle-Age, Baroque, Renaissance, or Romantic-period musical performances; or any theater piece that's toured or touring and can already be seen in any part of the Netherlands. An average of thirty-six productions per fest make the grade.

Fees: Not applicable.

Selection Criteria: Although many highly esteemed artists headline here, there is a good amount of opportunity for lesser known (but seasoned) pros. Scouts from this fest check out work all over the globe, and hook up with theater professionals in numerous countries to learn about exciting artist prospects, so if you know someone who knows someone, your chances of acceptance can greatly improve.

Payments/Profits/Benefits: Inquire about current guidelines if selected.

Physical Production Details: Productions are assigned theaters within the city of and vicinity of Amsterdam. These spaces include the mainstage Festival Centre in the Stadsschouwburg on Leidseplein, plus the Royal Carre Theatre, Muziektheater, the Tropical Museum and Tropical Theatre, the Paradiso, the Netherlands Film Museum and others.

Housing: Inquire about availability if selected.

Past Artists/Productions of Note: Peter Sellars, the Wooster Group, Romeo Castellucci.

Festival Flavor: Very intellectually stimulating. Artistic director Ivo van Hove has based his personal vision for the fest on melding art and art history as a gateway toward future creative accomplishment, inspired in his thinking by Kafka. Over 100,000 smart, open-minded audiences (about 60 percent of which are made up of locals) flock to the presentations.

The Bottom Line: Widely respected and recognized as one of the world's best boundary-pushing showcases.

Israel Festival, Israel

Founded: 1961

Contact Info: Israel Festival, 20 Marcus Street, PO Box 4409, Jerusalem, 91044, Israel
+972 (0) 561 1438 (phone); +972 (0) 2 566 9850 (fax)
E-mail: Israel_f@zahav.net.il

Web site: *www.euro-festival.net*

Performance Dates: Annually for one to three weeks in May-June.

The Festival's Mission: To strongly emphasize cultural harmony by blending the very best Israeli performing arts pieces with theater, opera, dance, and music offerings from all over the world.

Application Specifics: In 2003, the powder-keg political situation in Israel forced the festival's personnel to opt out of an international program temporarily; only Israeli artists were selected to present work. As one of the festival's primary traditional aims is to merge arts culture from all corners of the globe, however, this kind of artistic curtailment is made only when security concerns warrant. If you are an international artist, contact the festival for up-to-the-minute information on the program's status before sending a proposal; Israeli artists should contact for up-to-date proposal specifics.

Fees: Not applicable.

Selection Criteria: The Israel Festival often seeks out work that combines different creative disciplines in unprecedented ways. For instance, a highly regarded production from the Hebrew-Arab Theatre melded two short plays with choir performance. Another hallmark involves vividly breaking the fourth wall: Director Muni Yosef's play *Yisraela Shlomo* was staged to encourage actual confrontation and debate between its performers and its audience.

Payments/Profits/Benefits: Inquire about arrangements if selected.

Past Artists/Productions of Note: Pablo Casals, Bill Reilly, the Vienna State Opera, the dance/performance troupe Dollbeat.

Festival Flavor: The impact of this festival is very dominant—essentially, the entire country is proudly swept up in the excitement of the proceedings. Media coverage is extremely generous, as interest is so keen. This fest is also quite democratic in terms of making itself as accessible as possible; although many performances are ticketed, many are also free to the public. Hebrew is the principal language spoken, but English is also a strong part of the mix here; the local *Jerusalem Post* newspaper even prints a complete festival guide in English. There's great opportunity here to exchange ideas with artists and audience members, so attend all the shows you can.

The Bottom Line: An artistically impeccable fest with the noblest of intentions. If your work is top of the line, this fest is a completely enriching opportunity. Bear in mind, though: Your personal safety is paramount in this conflicted part of the world. Pay very close attention to world events, travel advisories, and word from the fest itself before you commit to attend or perform.

International Istanbul Theatre Festival, Turkey

Founded: 1989

Contact Info: Dikmen Gurun, director, Istanbul Foundation for Culture and Arts, Ystiklal Dadessi, Luur, Apt. No. 146, 80070-Beyoalu, Ystanbul/Turkey
+90 (212) 334 07 00 extension 738-740 (phone)
+90 (212) 334 07 05 (fax)

E-mail: theatre.fest@istfest.org

Web site: *www.istfest.org*

Performance Dates: Annually since its inception for about two weeks in May-June; beginning in 2005, the fest has plans to alternate with the International Ystanbul Biennial program.

The Festival's Mission: The fest was inaugurated as a way to give a shot in the arm to the sleeping giant that was quality Turkish theater. Its organization not only reinvigorated the homefront creative arts scene, but it became such a success that a major thrust now is to encourage collaborations and co-productions between Turkish artists and the world theater community.

Application Specifics: Inquire about current guidelines. The festival selects its "foreign guests" on the basis of strong reputation, but there are opportunities to be had even for young artists (via the New Voice program, which spotlights theatre and dance innovation through the work of emerging solo performers and companies).

Fees: Inquire about current guidelines.

Selection Criteria: Work that deals with the turbulent drama of immigration and finding one's home is a recent dominant theme. Oral history and poetry, dealing with personal experiences within the scope of global and social issues, is also often presented. Additionally, new reworkings/reimaginings of Greek tragedies have found a receptive audience here. Multi-lingual work abounds.

Payments/Profits/Benefits: Inquire about details if selected.

Physical Production Details: Extremely sophisticated production capabilities. Robert Wilson's *The Day Before* was staged here in all its technical glory; venues are generous in terms of space, and complicated multimedia pieces are a specialty.

Housing: Inquire about availability if selected.

Past Artists/Productions of Note: Co-productions with the Attis Theatre of Greece and the Japan Arts Center, among others; distinguished participating playmakers have included Mustaffa Aukyran, Thomas Ostermeier, and Wim Vanderkeybus.

Festival Flavor: This festival offers fantastic enrichment and networking opportunities for foreign artists through an extensive, impressive array of conferences, exhibitions, and workshops. Turkish artists are not only known to be artistically generous in terms of sharing their own knowledge and skills, but they strongly desire to learn from and embrace talented playmakers from outside cultures. So if your work excels, you might just find yourself getting the full-on rock star treatment.

The Bottom Line: A rare chance to experience both creative and cultural riches in a supportive and stimulating environment.

Ko Festival of Performance at Amherst (KoFest)

Founded: 1991

Contact Info: Contact Ko TheatreWorks, Inc., the sponsoring organization, preferably through e-mail at info@kofest.com, or at (413) 427-6147 (phone).

Web site: *www.Kofest.com*

Performance Dates: Annually for five weeks in July-August.

The Festival's Mission: Sabrina Hamilton, artistic director, co-founded Ko Fest with friends she'd performed experimental theater with. "We felt that maybe we could create a friendlier place for artists to tour to, as we'd been on the road a lot ourselves and had learned about some of the problems of being on the road," she recalls. "At the beginning, we produced our own work, and then we also invited people we knew in to perform as well. It's very much about working in a collaborative manner, across disciplines, across genres. There's absolutely no house style, in that we can always tell audiences, 'If you don't like the show this week, come next week!'"

Application Specifics: "We also have a program of rehearsal residencies, where people can come and work on pieces but not have to perform them. Sometimes, those pieces may end up in the festival the following year," says Hamilton. "So that's one way for people whom I don't know, or whose work I haven't seen, to have a little bit of a look-see, and that lets me know much more about whether I'm interested in it for the following year." Inquire for up-to-date rehearsal residency info and guidelines.

Fees: If you want to participate in an affiliated workshop (past hands-on topics have included acting, the dramaturgy of community, and making theater pieces out of documentary resources), you'll pay $300.

Selection Criteria: In terms of artists she chooses, Hamilton offers, "A lot of them are people that I know, or people who know the festival who recommend people. Some of it is stuff that I just go see—there are venues where I feel there's compatible stuff, you know, the sort of PS 122s of the world. Also, I've had people approach me all the way from Russia, who I've never heard of before. Sometimes I'll put artists together—people who don't know each other, and who are missing a component."

Payments/Profits/Benefits: It varies. It's basically a combination of flat fee, box-office split, or special monies allocated in certain circumstances for a foreign company's expenses, for example). Inquire about specifics if selected.

Physical Production Details: The festival utilizes the facilities at Amherst College Studio Theatre, with sophisticated light and sound; two to three rehearsal spaces; and twenty-four-hour-a-day access to all theater spaces. (Upon occasion, Ko Fest has used Hampshire College facilities as well.) Within all of these spaces, Hamilton's long career as a lighting designer informs a great deal of developmental work: "Sometimes we have people into the festival who have not had access to sophisticated lighting. One of the things I do a lot of is using the process of lighting the piece as a way of sort of developing it dramaturgically, in clarifying the work, giving toeholds to the audience through the process of that visual design element." Tech time is generous and often available on Monday for a show that won't go up till Friday. Outdoor performances have also taken place on the lawn of the Amherst observatory.

Housing: Provided in the Amherst dorms for all participants.

Past Artists/Productions of Note: Cornerstone Theatre Company, The Ghost Road Company, Sandglass Theatre, Touchstone Theater, and many others.

Festival Flavor: "Sometimes we've had a thing called the Critics' Project, where we invite critics or scholars into the rehearsal process, so that they can see how more experimental work is made," says Hamilton. "A lot of people in working in that field really don't have any idea how the well-made play is put together or developed. It also gives the artists sometimes a very interesting perspective on their work as it's in development. Sometimes those collaborations even stuck. We had one person in for the Critics' Project, and she ended up being a dramaturg for a piece that was in rehearsal residency, and stuck with the piece even after she had left the environment."

The Bottom Line: The very definition of excellent performance-driven work is always found here.

Hip-Hop Theater Festivals (New York City & San Francisco)

Founded: NYC fest, 2000; SF fest, 2003

Contact Info: Mona Baroudi, Yerba Buena Center for the Arts (YBCA), 701 Mission Street, San Francisco, CA 94103 (415) 321-1307 (phone)

E-mail: mbaroudi@yerbabuenaarts.org

Web site: *www.yerbabuenaarts.org*

Performance Dates: NYC fest, annually for approximately twenty days in June; SF fest, initial preview held in September 2003, fest debut in spring 2004.

The Festivals' Mission: To introduce the art of hip-hop to the general public, and reach out to young people, relating plots, characters, music, and movement to their lives.

Application Specifics: Currently, the NYC fest has no Web site with application specifics, so direct questions regarding getting your work considered to the YBCA. For all artists submitting work for any project at YBCA, staffers ask for a videotape of work, a resume, and a self-addressed, stamped envelope (send to the attention of the Performing Arts Curator).

Fees: Inquire about latest guidelines.

Selection Criteria: Very high. The world's best hip-hop playwrights, performers, and dancers only are spotlighted through the festivals, like Will Power, the Hip-Hop Theater Junction Melina Corazon Foley, and Jonzi D.

Payments/Profits/Benefits: Inquire if asked to take part.

Physical Production Details: The two revered PS 122 spaces in Manhattan are home to the NYC fest. In San Francisco, the main space used for the three-day September 2003 preview fest was the YBCA's Forum, a multi-purpose venue configured for everything from performance to symposiums.

Housing: Inquire if asked to take part.

Past Artists/Productions of Note: *Surface Transit* by Sarah Jones; *Jails, Hospitals, and Hip-Hop* by Danny Hoch.

Festival Flavor: Highly professional—the NYC fest is now sponsored by *Vibe* magazine.

The Bottom Line: For established hip-hop playwrights and performers, the finest showcases available. If you're an emerging artist, inquire about the possibility of working here, but be realistic about the high caliber of participants.

Lincoln Center Festival

Founded: 1996

Contact Info: Lincoln Center for the Performing Arts, Administrative Offices, 70 Lincoln Plaza, New York, NY

(212) 875-5000 (phone)

Web site: *www.lincolncenter.org*

Performance Dates: Annually each summer.

The Festival's Mission: To laud both Western and non-Western classical traditions in theater, opera, multimedia, dance, chamber music, and multidisciplinary creative endeavors.

Application Specifics: If you are a world-class artist on the level of Nakamura Kankuro V, master Kabuki thespian (whose esteemed work the festival has featured recently), then this is the forum for you. If not, don't be naïve enough to submit a performance video! Instead, immerse yourself in studying performances at the festival, and check out the Lincoln Center Web site to become involved in one of the organization's many educational programs to get your feet wet.

Fees: Not applicable.

Selection Criteria: Only the most accomplished artists are invited to present work.

Payments/Profits/Benefits: Not applicable unless you are a selected artist making individual, confidential arrangements with the festival.

Physical Production Details: Theater performance spaces include the New York State Theater, the John Jay College Theater, and Alice Tully Hall. Additional festival venues include the Metropolitan Opera House.

Housing: Not applicable unless you are a selected artist making individual, confidential arrangements with the festival.

Past Artists/Productions of Note: Not just traditional in their style or approach—recent participating artists have included Elvis Costello, DJ Spooky, That Subliminal Kid, and Mikhail Barishnikov (acting in the innovative drama *Forbidden Christmas or The Doctor and the Patient*).

Festival Flavor: Thrilling, enlightening, stimulating.

The Bottom Line: Arguably the best performance festival on earth.

Midtown International Theatre Festival

Founded: 1999

Contact Info: Contact this festival ONLY through e-mail: festival@oobr.com

The festival takes place in New York City at the Midtown International Theatre Festival Annex, 347 West 36th Street.

Performance Dates: Annually for a little over two weeks in
July-August.

The Festival's Mission: John Chatterton, publisher/editor of the
popular theater periodical *Off-Off Broadway Review*, started
this festival in order to spotlight the plentiful Manhattan
stage talent he'd become so familiar with. The fest, which
accepts full productions only, has since expanded in a geographical sense, including work from as far away as Australia.

Application Specifics: Check out the application form at the
Web site address above. In addition to submitting the com-
pleted form, you must also provide a cover letter, project
synopsis, full script, a videotape of the project if available
(this is mandatory if you're proposing a solo show), bios of
everybody who's collaborating with you, an audiotape of the
project's score if it's a musical, and relevant reviews/PR.
(You do submit *this* package via regular mail to: Midtown
International Theatre Festival, 347 W. 36th St., #1204, NY,
NY 10018.)

Fees: If you're chosen to participate, there's a non-refundable fee
of $300 for companies, or $150 for solo productions. Each
company pays its own expenses entirely.

Selection Criteria: This fest frowns upon gimmicky premises
further spiced up with sexy titles. Thoughtful material,
diverse in its sexual and racial themes, is appreciated instead.
All genres considered. Approximately forty-five plays are chosen per year. Additionally, your proposal will be judged from
a business standpoint: The fest wants your production to run
self-sufficiently, and therefore will evaluate your producer's
credentials and marketing ideas carefully. (The fest does do
quite a bit of general promotion, but also expects each
production to endeavor to fill its own seats.)

Payments/Profits/Benefits: Each show is designated a minimum
number of tickets that should be sold per performance. If
this quota isn't met, the show owes the festival nothing.

If, however, the show exceeds its minimum sales, the show's personnel splits the excess revenue above that number with the festival. If a show is picked up by a commercial producer, the festival will make no claim on future revenue or royalties. (FYI: This festival's proximity to the Broadway theater district makes being seen by major movers and shakers very possible for those companies who solicit.) Post-show audience surveys also provide instant feedback on every production.

Physical Production Details: No show can be longer than an hour and a half; a list of costumes and props must be given to the festival production manager; storage space is assigned and set pieces are shared by shows; set-up/strikes can be no longer than a half-hour; there's a general lighting plot that cannot be played around with. Each company provides its own light/sound techie, and the festival's technical adviser will run an instrument and sound check at the start of each show run day. One blocking and one tech rehearsal in-space is scheduled for each production.

Housing: Not provided.

Past Artists/Productions of Note: *American Story*.

Festival Flavor: These folks are admirably no-nonsense. They treat this festival like the serious business it is, and don't suffer fools gladly. You'll be required to attend meetings and curb your cast's egos if necessary; interference with schedule times or tech or set matters can cause your company to be fined.

The Bottom Line: A fabulous opportunity to showcase your work in the Big Apple.

Piccolo Spoleto

Founded: 1979

Contact Info: Contact this fest through phone: (843)-724-7305
e-mail: cultural_affairs@ci.charleston.sc.us

Web site: *www.ci.charleston.sc.us*

Performance Dates: Annually every May-June for seventeen days.

The Festival's Mission: To act as an artists' outreach from the grand Spoleto festival, cultivating and presenting the work of performing, literary, and visual artists mainly from the Southwest. Geared very distinctly toward kids.

Application Specifics: E-mail fest at above address for current requirements.

Fees: E-mail fest at above address for current requirements.

Selection Criteria: A haven for quirky, cutting-edge, original theater.

Payments/Profits/Benefits: Inquire about current guidelines.

Physical Production Details: Nearly 100 wildly varied performance sites, ranging from traditional theater and auditorium spaces to churches, bars, parks, museums, a city jail, and a Starbucks.

Housing: Not provided.

Past Artists/Productions of Note: *JOB: The Hip-Hop Musical*; *One-Man Star Wars Trilogy*; *One-Man Lord of the Rings Trilogy*

Festival Flavor: Vibrant and exciting. In addition to over 700 arts performances, festival artists and festival-goers can mingle and enjoy themselves at a reggae dance, concerts, and an adjunct kids' festival.

The Bottom Line: Don't miss it.

The Rainbow Theater Festival (Bread & Water Theatre)

Founded: 1999; reconfigured in 2003

Contact Info: Jason R. Teeter, Artistic Director, Bread & Water Theatre, 20 Alpine Lane, Caledonia, NY 14423

E-mail: info@breadandwatertheatre.org

Web site: *www.breadandwatertheatre.org*

Performance Dates: Typically four full productions and two staged readings, annually in January-February.

The Festival's Mission: The Rainbow Theater Festival's first incarnation was as a student organization at Nazareth College; its initial purpose was to serve as a touchstone for the gay and lesbian community. When Jason Teeter reformed the fest as a professional offshoot of the Bread and Water Theatre with Marcy J. Savastano, Mario J. Savastano, Carl Girard, and West End director/SM David Henderson, however, adjustments occurred. "I changed the focus of the festival from general queer issues to the Rainbow Pride Flag," says Teeter. "Each color of the Rainbow Flag represents a different facet of queer life. The color/meanings are as follows: pink (sexuality), red (life), orange (healing), yellow (sun), green (natural), turquoise (art), indigo (harmony), and violet (spirit). The colors pink and turquoise would later be removed from the Rainbow flag due to production constraints." Festival subject matter focuses each year on a different color thematically. Teeter also insisted that straight men and women be included in the fest in order to promote the message of acceptance and universality, plus created "The Lamda Project," a program that fuses real-life stories into performance pieces.

Application Specifics: Contact Teeter at the above address for current needs/guidelines.

Fees: Not applicable.

Selection Criteria: Teeter's artistic wish list includes material that facilitates more community outreach. "I would so much like to do children's theatre geared to the children of gay and lesbian parents," he says.

Payments/Profits/Benefits: Stipends/salaries paid only to company members.

Physical Production Details: No permanent venue—the festival takes place in a variety of spaces, typical of which has been a local pub space (about fifty seats, a 30 feet wide by 50 feet deep stage). As a rule, the fest uses minimal set and tech, employing the in-house audio of any given venue and incorporating portable lighting towers.

Housing: Not provided.

Past Artists/Productions of Note: Teeter praises the playwriting skill of his associate Mario Savastano, and the directing skill of his colleague Carl Girard, who present consistently acclaimed work at the festival. Memorable past productions have included adaptations of *The Yellow Wallpaper* by Charlotte Perkins Gilman and *The Little Prince*, based on the novella by Antoine de Saint-Exupery.

Festival Flavor: "The greatest achievement is the creation of self-esteem within our audience," says Teeter. "Much of the Rainbow Theater Festival is building people up, helping them feel comfortable in their own skin by giving them stories they can relate to." Teeter recalls that during one festival, a group of his actors performed a series of one-acts for kids in the youth program of GAGV, the Gay Alliance of the Genesee Valley, New York. "Not used to live theatre, this audience cheered at things they liked and took so much joy at seeing 'themselves' up onstage. After the show we got to meet our audience, and their hugs and encouragement meant so much to me," he enthuses. "Only at that point did I feel like had done something important, and that I had changed lives!"

The Bottom Line: A great place to do impactful, important work.

Seattle Festival of Improv Theater

Founded: 2002

Contact Info: Seattle Festival of Improv Theater, c/o Historic University Theater, 5510 University Way NE, Seattle, WA 98105-3521

(206) 781-3952 (phone)

E-mail: mattg@seattleimprov.com

Web site: *www.seattleimprov.com*

Performance Dates: Annually in February.

The Festival's Mission: Matt Grabowski, the fest's founder, is
    a seasoned performer himself, and knows the improv scenes
    of New York and Chicago like the back of his hand. When he
    moved to Seattle several years ago, he says, "What I found
    was a very large community of improvisers who were really,
    for the most part, ten to twenty years behind what was going
    in New York and Chicago. From my perspective, it wasn't
    work that was on the same quality level as work that I was
    used to seeing in other parts of the country." Hooking up
    with Jet City Improv head Andrew McMasters, Grabowski
    got financial backing from that well-known organization.
    "The mission was really to bring people from New York and
    Chicago to Seattle to show people what was really going on,"
    he recalls. This fest now seeks to position itself on an interna-
    tional level, and further works to put Seattle on the map in
    terms of being identified with great improv performance.

Application Specifics: Inquire about latest guidelines.
    Unsolicited tapes are accepted; Grabowski often catches
    live performances as well.

Fees: Not applicable.

Selection Criteria: "Every group has a style—there are even
    regional styles, flavors of improv that you can tell if you
    watch enough of this stuff," says Grabowski. "And they're
    pretty distinctive if you know what to look for. Personally,
    what I look for in terms of performers is, do they look like
    they belong on a stage? Do they have vocal technique? Do
    they have physical technique? The same kinds of things
    you'd look for in any actor. Especially in improvisers, there's
    so many people who get into improv as amateurs and never
    aspire to be anything but amateurs. I want a group that looks
    good onstage and that has the acting talent. You can also tell
    improv technique. There are different 'rules' that people use
    when they perform improv. I don't really believe in that, but

you can kind of tell when people have technique and when they don't. And then just, is it different? Is this something I've seen a hundred times before, or are these guys doing something they've obviously put some time into and developed together over a period of time?"

Payments/Profits/Benefits: Inquire about current guidelines.

Physical Production Details: Two venues have housed the fest: the Historic University Theater, and the Market Theater. "Your tech, if you're lucky—we can probably do an afternoon on Friday, if you can get your whole group out here by that time in order to do whatever tech you need. We can definitely arrange short rehearsals."

Housing: Inquire about availability if selected.

Past Artists/Productions of Note: *Johnny Lunchpail; Scooby-Doo; The Josh & Tamra Show* (a puppet show featured often on *Late Night with Conan O'Brien*)

Festival Flavor: "I wanted to really make our performers available to our audience, so for both years that we've done it, we've had a big party on the closing night of the festival," says Grabowski. "We've also kind of planned these other events, like going to a bar one night; we had an opening night party. The idea is basically, hey, any audience members who want to come and hang out with these guys, let's be rock stars! Let's make ourselves available to our audience so they can bask in it, participate in it, be like, 'Hey, I was hanging out with this dude from Chicago who's a really great performer and so much fun!'"

The Bottom Line: An emerging powerhouse in the world of improv theater.

Spoleto Festival USA

Founded: 1977

Contact Info: Spoleto Festival USA, PO Box 157, Charleston, SC 29402-0157
(843) 722–2764 (phone); (843) 723–6383 (fax)

Web site: *www.spoletousa.org*

Performance Dates: Annually each spring for seventeen days.

The Festival's Mission: Founded by Gian Carlo Menotti, Christopher Keene, and their associates from Italy's legendary Festival of Two Worlds in Spoleto, Italy, Spoleto USA was intended as its American counterpart. The thrust of Spoleto USA is, as in Europe, to give young artists the chance to work with masters—and also to bring the community of Charleston an international array of excellent established and emerging talent. The festival includes theater, opera, musical theater, dance, visual arts, lectures, and additional events. Nigel Redden, Spoleto's director, elaborates: "When the festival was begun, it was possible—perhaps even desirable—for an arts organization simply to march to the drum of artistic integrity, of artistic innovation, of artistic excitement. By the late nineties, it became additionally about building a community—how one integrates with the community. I think to some extent, this is perhaps a sign of maturity, a sign of change in the arts."

Application Specifics: Spoleto only presents talent by invitation. Its companion festival, Piccolo Spoleto, however, does accept unsolicited talent (see separate directory listing).

Fees: Not applicable.

Selection Criteria: "I think obviously there are many people involved in the artistic program here," says Redden. "I think the theme that runs through all the work is that someone here has to be passionate about it. I am not necessarily passionate about everything, although I am passionate about a fair amount of what we do. But if I'm not passionate, somebody's got to be passionate. It's not a question of looking in some kind of catalogue from a manager and saying, Okay, we'll have one of these, one of those, and one of these other things. What it is, is a question of saying, so-and-so's dancing enormously well at the moment—it would be wonderful to have him or her."

Payments/Profits/Benefits: Confidentially arranged between artists and the festival.

Physical Production Details: Spoleto's performances happen all over Charleston; venues range from theaters to churches to the local college campus to the grounds of the Middleton Place plantation.

Housing: Confidentially arranged between artists and the festival.

Past Artists/Productions of Note: *The American Clock* by Arthur Miller; *Creve Coeur* by Tennessee Williams; *Hydrogen Jukebox* by Phillip Glass and Alan Ginsberg; *Empty Places* by Laurie Anderson.

Festival Flavor: Regarding the flow of festival feedback, Redden comments, "Obviously, I talk to artists a lot, but I don't feel I'm bringing them back information from an audience. I think I'm bringing them back information from myself. I think that audiences are important to some artists; somewhat irrelevant to others. I can't believe that anyone is a performer and doesn't care about some kind of reaction on the other side of the footlights; I don't think they're doing it simply for themselves, the way that a painter might. But that being said, I feel that the best feedback is, if I can continue to do it. Obviously, you can't continue if you don't pay your bills. I don't believe that paying bills is my purpose in doing this . . . but if you don't pay your bills, you can't get things onstage, so at some point you have to do it. My feeling is that as long as people are prepared to come in sufficient numbers, and donors are prepared to give us sufficient amounts of money so we can continue doing it, I believe that that's the feedback I need."

The Bottom Line: See and learn from everything you can here. Then think about trying Piccolo Spoleto, to get your feet wet and your talent known locally.

Viladecans International Theatre and Animation Festival, Spain

Founded: 1989

Contact Info: Contact festival manager Rafael Salinas through the fest's Web site.

Web site: *www.atriumviladecans.com*

The Festival's Mission: To celebrate street theater. Performances encompass traditional plays plus dance, circus, musical, and animated presentations, staged throughout Viladecans, a Barcelona suburb.

Application Specifics: The fest is open to international companies and solo performers of all stripes. Contact the fest to find out up-to-date submission guidelines.

Fees: Inquire about current guidelines.

Selection Criteria: Unjuried, open, and unrestricted. Although Spanish is dominantly spoken, performers may work in any language they like, as well as in any genre they like. Keep in mind that you'll have to compete to get noticed, though; virtually every inch of the city will be covered by working artists. Viladecans's citizens, dignitaries, and tourists stroll through the hubbub of clashing simultaneous works and pick and choose what they want to watch.

Payments/Profits/Benefits: Financially, minimal. All performances are free to the public, so don't expect to get rich. Clear buskering with the fest before you put out your open money jar to make sure you're absolutely complying with current rules. Career-wise, though, you could clean up. A super perk this fest offers is an annual professional contacts fair, where networking for future work can happen, so bring lots of business cards (in Spanish if you speak it, as well as in English).

Physical Production Details: Some performers simply grab whatever street corner they can. Others work in gardens, street squares, or buildings converted into makeshift stages.

Housing: Not provided.

Past Artists/Productions of Note: *The Imaginary Patient; Them Rollerockets; This is My History; The Celebration of the Crazy People.*

Festival Flavor: Raw, vibrant, and wild. Be advised to do your homework beforehand in regard to lodging—this festival is wildly popular, so the best (and safest) places to stay will book up far in advance. A working knowledge of Spanish is strongly recommended. Also, transportation can be a tricky proposition; cabs cost a fortune, so you'll probably have to resort to figuring out the train system from Barcelona, or try your luck using the public bus system. The reason this is somewhat challenging is you have to tell the difference between regular and "fast trains," the latter of which won't get you to the fest (ask a local for help).

The Bottom Line: An exhilarating adventure, both creatively and as a life experience.

Section 3

Playwrights' Festivals

Attic Theatre Ensemble's One-Act Marathon

Founded: 1993

Contact Info: Attic Theatre Ensemble, Attn: Literary Manager, 5429 W. Washington Blvd., Los Angeles, CA 90016-1112 (323) 734-8977 (phone)

E-mail: AtticTheatre1@aol.com

Web site: *www.AtticTheatre.org*

The Festival's Mission: Attic's overall goals include developing new works and playwrights, plus to use live stagework by its acting ensemble as a means to educate audiences; this fest is one of the ways they fulfill these intentions.

Application Specifics: All genres considered, but work should be geared toward mature audiences. Forty-five minutes is the max running time; work must be unproduced, wholly original, and copyrighted to the author (no adaptations). Mail complete script with a short synopsis, character breakdown, your resume/bio, and a cover letter with contact information. A required submission form is available at the Web site address above.

Fees: A $15 registration and processing fee must accompany all submissions, and it's non-refundable.

Selection Criteria: Six to twelve scripts are picked for full production in the festival. How they're whittled down: All submitted scripts are evaluated by three different company members, then graded on a number of factors ranging from strength of plot to dialogue and character arc. Scripts that score well move on to the finalist round, where the material is examined for production-worthiness (you could get a full production, or you could get a staged reading).

Payments/Profits/Benefits: A panel of Attic Theatre associates will judge all marathon finalists, and there are two cash prizes: $250 for the winner, and $100 for the runner-up. In past years, the third-place script has received another full production as well. Attic's policy has been to take a six-month window for scripts winning first to six places for exclusive option—the company has many avenues it pursues in terms of further film and play production.

Physical Production Details: The Jewel Theatre Center offers the Jewel Box performance space; contact company for more information, or check out the Web site for up-to-date tech specs.

Housing: If chosen, inquire about availability.

Past Artists/Productions of Note: *Something Spanish* by Saul Zachary; *Life Support* by Donald Steele.

Festival Flavor: Attic artistic director James Carey is not only a very nice guy, but he's very encouraging when it comes to artists who strive to take bold risks. He stays personally familiar with the latest material of writers he likes, with a view toward forging long-term collaboration.

The Bottom Line: Considered one of the best companies in Los Angeles for emerging talent.

Baltimore Playwrights' Festival

Founded: 1981

Contact Info: Mark Scharf, Chairman, Baltimore Playwrights Festival, 251 S. Ann Street, Baltimore, Maryland 21231

E-mail: librarian@baltplayfest.org

Web site: *www.baltplayfest.org*

Performance Dates: Annually in July.

The Festival's Mission: To stimulate production of talented local playwrights.

Application Specifics: Open to current/previous residents of Maryland or those who currently work or have previously worked in Maryland. All submitted plays must be unproduced. Mail three copies of your play (with a brief synopsis in each copy). Make two title pages: one with full contact information, and the second only listing the title of your play (plays are read anonymously to discourage any form of favoritism). Also, if your script is a musical, submit the score on audiotape. Small cast sizes recommended. One-acts should run no longer than an hour, and full-lengths no longer than two and a half hours.

Fees: A $5 submission fee.

Selection Criteria: "I would love to bring in a musical," says Mark Scharf, award-winning playwright and chairman of the festival. "I know people who write musicals, and that is such a tough thing, to attempt a musical here. I think that would be really exciting." He believes, refreshingly, that playwrights should have the final say over how their work is presented. "The BPF has guidelines written down for playwrights and directors—you cannot change (the play) without the playwright's permission. I think that is extremely important to set that out, because I've been involved in festivals—I've shown up opening night once, and the last line (I wrote) was cut. I went backstage and none of the actors would look at me. I said, 'I thought it was kind of important!' The director just cut it. I said, 'Don't you think you should have talked to me first?' So that can't happen. We're not writing movies; we're not hired hands; we're not employees." Scharf's compassion for other writers informs the way this fest is run in every facet of operation.

Payment/Profits/Benefits: Inquire about current policy if selected.

Physical Production Details: Only minimal set pieces are used.

Housing: Not applicable.

Past Artists/Productions of Note: In addition to Scharf, festival alumni include Kathleen Barber, Joe Dennison, Chris Dickerson, and many others.

Festival Flavor: This festival fosters an atmosphere of great support and camaraderie. "The community of playwrights that have been involved with the festival over time—there is a core that know each other, and show up for each others' work, and it's just lovely," says Scharf. "All those clichés you hear about theater people—it's just the exact opposite."

The Bottom Line: A very nurturing environment for local writers.

Bay Area Playwrights' Festival

Founded: 1976

Contact Info: Christine Young, Literary Manager, The Playwrights Foundation, 131 10th Street, 3rd Floor, San Francisco, CA 94103 (415) 626-0453 (phone); (415) 626-1138 (fax)

E-mail: admin@playwrightsfoundation.org

Web site: *www.playwrightfoundation.org*

Performance Dates: Annually for two weeks in July-August.

The Festival's Mission: To help emerging American playwrights hone their work and to bring this work to the stage for current and future audiences.

Application Specifics: Submit full script with resume and cover letter (with your e-mail address) with self-addressed, stamped envelope by mail. BFA and MFA students are also welcome to include a letter of recommendation. Scripts must be full-length, original, and unproduced.

Fees: None.

Selection Criteria: Some weight is given to the fact that a writer is from the Bay Area, but that's far less important than high quality. This festival is one of the country's most prestigious forums for important, cutting-edge material, lots of it politically, socially, and emotionally charged. All genres considered—just make sure your work is up to snuff. Six to eight plays will be chosen for the festival, at which dramaturgs will work on the material with the writer.

Payments/Profits/Benefits: A stipend, plus travel expenses. The prestige factor speaks for itself.

Physical Production Details: Varied venues, including the Magic Theatre, A Traveling Jewish Theater, the Z Space, The Marsh, and Intersection for the Arts. Before final performances, there are two rehearsed readings (between which there are production breaks for author rewrites).

Housing: Provided—details given if you're chosen for the festival.

Past Artists/Productions of Note: The great Sam Shepard ignited the inaugural festival with *The Sad Lament of Pecos Bill on the Eve of Killing His Wife*, his trailblazing rock opera. Other esteemed artists whose work has graced this fest include Anna Deveare Smith, Nilo Cruz, Robert Alexander, David Henry Hwang, Claire Chafee, and many, many others. Tony, Obie, and Pulitzer Prize winners abound on the alumni list (over 250 playwrights strong).

Festival Flavor: Artistic Director Amy Mueller is known for her dedication to and support of new writers. Mueller's generosity infuses such ventures as New Play Resources, a program affiliated with the festival that hooks up playwrights with compatible theaters.

The Bottom Line: Make sure your credentials are as strong as your writing before giving this fest a go. Approach them once you've had several plays produced at respected theaters—you want to make your best impression.

Boston Theater Marathon

Founded: 1999

Contact Info: Attn: Boston Theater Marathon, Boston Playwrights' Theatre, 949 Commonwealth Avenue, Boston, MA 02215 (617) 353-5899 (phone)

Web site: *www.bu.edu/btm/index.html*

Performance Dates: Annually one Sunday in April.

The Festival's Mission: According to the Marathon's artistic director, Kate Snodgrass, "A friend of mine, Bill Lattanzi, and I were both playwrights. We'd been talking for a long time about how difficult it was to get plays done, and for producers to read plays, and how to manage getting to know a theater company when you didn't. We had talked about that for a long time, and one day, we came up with a viable idea, in my mind. I had been associated with an all-day marathon of plays with Circle Rep years ago, and I wanted to do something like that. Talking to Bill, we decided that what we needed to do was put a different theater company with each play, so that the playwrights could manage to get with a theater company and no one theater company would benefit—everybody would benefit."

Application Specifics: Only New England authors are eligible (and may submit a maximum of two plays apiece, including collaborations). All plays must run ten minutes or less (a max of ten pages). All genres considered. Submit three copies of your play, plus, on a separate title page, full contact info. Plays are read anonymously by different readers. Plays are narrowed down to a round of 100 finalists, which are read by another three different readers, who choose from these the

Marathon's presentations. Some writers, such as David Mamet, have been asked to put work in the Marathon.

Fees: None.

Selection Criteria: "Last year we got about 330 entries, this year, over 300," says Snodgrass. "One year we produced as many as 50, but now we're pretty much leveled out at 46. When I'm reading, I look for speakable dialogue and an intelligent writer who seems to know what the theater is. And that runs the gamut, from Beckett to Pirandello to Lanford Wilson. So I try to be as open as I can to possibilities, because I never know what those last three readers are going to gravitate to. And it's different every year."

Payments/Profits/Details: All festival profits go to charity, so the artistic and networking benefits are your reward—and quite plentiful. "There have been some times when the theater companies have really liked their playwrights, and asked to read longer works, and their playwrights have been produced. This has happened two or three times in six years," says Snodgrass.

Physical Production Benefits: Here's the killer schedule in a nutshell: Approximately forty plays are performed by forty separate companies two times in one ten-hour day. The Marathon runs on two stages at Boston University. Each theater company gets a half-hour rehearsal in each space. (At press time, the Marathon had booked space for its next fest at the Huntington Theatre Company.) Shows set up and strike very rapidly; only very minimal props or set pieces are used.

Housing: Not applicable.

Past Artists/Productions of Note: Loads of great work, including *Chekov on Ice* by Robert Brustein, presented by the American Repertory Theatre; *Speedbag* by Israel Horovitz, presented by the Gloucester Stage Company/Theatre Redux; *Chance of Your Life* by Brandon Toropov, presented by Portland Stage Company; *The Actress* by Theresa Rebeck, presented by the Huntington Theatre Company.

Festival Flavor: The Marathon is a must-attend event for local theater pros. "I think a lot of the Boston theater community shows up because it's exciting, and they want to see each other's work," Snodgrass feels. The Marathon is highly respected by the Boston media; the local press often does advance articles, which help promote the fest, and Snodgrass's staff does a strong advertising push as well.

The Bottom Line: A wonderful playwright's platform, plus an ideal place to watch your work performed by masters of the craft.

Brave New Works Festival

Founded: Circa 1990

Contact Info: Max Reimer, Artistic Director, Theater Aquarius, 190 King William Street, Hamilton, ON L8R 1A8, Canada (Carolyn Drost, Development and Education Coordinator) (905) 522-7815 X 328 (phone)

E-mail: cdrost@theatreaquarius.org

Web site: *www.theatreaquarious.org*

Performance Dates: Annually for four days in November.

The Festival's Mission: To develop scripts with a view toward making them as high-quality as possible. Nightly readings of selected scripts take place in front of an audience. Post-performance, Max Reimer leads a discussion about the work—stage-worthiness and audience suitability are among the developmental factors addressed. Audience members' feedback is a major component in helping to shape each script.

Application Specifics: All genres considered. Send full script and a cover letter with complete contact info to Reimer at the above address. If he is interested, he'll be in touch.

Fees: Not applicable.

Selection Criteria: Quality counts. Also good to know: Theatre Aquarius as an entity is dedicated to making theater accessible to the widest possible audience in their locale. Playwrights who live in Hamilton region or know it have a leg up for that reason.

Payments/Profits/Benefits: Primarily artistic; inquire about further development arrangements.

Physical Production Details: The fest readings take place in the theater's Founders' Lounge balcony space, not in the stage space.

Housing: Not generally applicable, as many participants are locals. Inquire if selected in regard to availability.

Past Artists/Productions of Note: Numerous playwrights who want to develop, rather than flat-out stage, their pieces—so this fest doesn't boast "name" participants or productions.

Festival Flavor: This fest's thrust is educational. Participating playwrights should understand going in that their work is going to be constructively criticized, and praised, by both theater aficionados and novices. Those with thin skin need not apply.

The Bottom Line: Very worthwhile if you know the local audience culture, and if you're open-minded enough to learn objectively about your script's strengths and weaknesses.

Coe College Playwriting Festival

Founded: 1993

Contact Info: Susan Wolverton, Festival Chair, Department of Theatre Arts, Coe College, 1220 First Avenue N.E., Cedar Rapids, IA 52402
(877) CALL COE (phone)

E-mail: swolvert@coe.edu

Web site: *www.coe.edu/academics/TheatreArts/events/htm*

Performance Dates: See Web site for most up-to-date information. Historically, biennially in January.

The Festival's Mission: To develop new plays, encourage key feedback to playwrights, and explore political, social, and ethical topics within an academic framework. Susan Wolverton, the festival's founder and director, says, "We initially had it as a festival and symposium, and had members of the community come in. It was more of a humanities lecture series, and that was part of getting funding

through the state. But we backed away from that—it just
seemed like more than we needed to do, and the play
was enough."

Application Specifics: U.S. citizens may submit original, unproduced, full-length plays on the theme posted on the fest's
Web site. Not considered: musicals, translated, or adapted
pieces, or multi-authored pieces. Include a synopsis and resume.

Fees: None.

Selection Criteria: "In terms of just looking at a play, it's kind
of just a gut thing after doing it for so many years," says
Woolverton. In terms of how work has been evaluated in past
years, she explains, "I guess the ones we were most attracted
to were pieces that really were theatrical. We get a lot of
pieces that read as if they're film pieces. They'd be really
good for film, but we really were looking for pieces that
could actually be done onstage. We're also looking for new
voices, not the standard. We get a lot of things from playwrights who have clearly been writing for a long time, and it's
kind of formula. We were also looking for work that really
broke out of those boundaries, those kinds of almost formu-
laic systems. Obviously, good writing. You get a sense for it."

Payment/Profits/Benefits: A staged reading, plus a $325 prize and
travel expenses. Playwrights get to work hands-on in classes
with Coe students as well.

Physical Production Details: Woolverton explains, "We've always
used our mainstage. It's not a typical proscenium mainstage—
it can be done in an arena, it can be done thrust. It's a little
mini-Guthrie, if that makes sense. It has an intimate feeling,
that space. And that's where the rehearsals were. In the earlier
versions of this festival, we'd do a whole week of rehearsals.
More recently, when my colleague Lisa Schlesinger has been
directing these, she's more interested in being really focused
on the language, but also keeping it fresh, so we wouldn't do
that many rehearsals, really. We're using people from the

college community or the Cedar Rapids community, a blend
of individuals who get involved, some of them actors, some of
them not necessarily actors. We do just simple lighting. They
might sit on chairs, or we might elevate a few people, no
movement really, using the script. Never any costumes or anything like that. Again, we really want to focus on hearing the
play; there's not a lot of distraction."

Housing: A week's room and board on the Coe campus is included
for the duration of the winning playwrights' residencies. Often,
playwrights are treated to dinners out as well.

Past Artists/Productions of Note: Jamie Pacino, whose monologues have been frequently published in student anthologies.

Festival Flavor: The intellectual give-and-take playwrights are
encouraged to have with students in an academic setting is rare
and valuable. "We do like them to talk to the students about
how they started," says Woolverton. "Some of them are really
into working with students one-on-one with their pieces; it
kind of depends on where the playwright is, how comfortable
they feel doing that. So those opportunities are there."

The Bottom Line: If you take a scholarly approach to your writing,
this is a fantastic opportunity to both hone your dramatic skills
and immerse yourself in intelligentsia.

Contemporary American Theater Festival

Founded: 1991

Contact Info: Ed Herendeen, Producing Director, Contemporary
American Theater Festival, P.O. Box 429, Shepherdstown,
West Virginia 25443
(304) 876-3473, (800) 999-CATF (phone)

Web site: *www.catf.org*

Performance Dates: Annually every July-August.

The Festival's Mission: "The Contemporary American Theater
Festival is dedicated to producing and developing new

American theater," explains Ed Herendeen. "Our core values are to sustain an artistic process of innovation and daring, to tell diverse stories, and to create a profound and ever-evolving relationship between the audience and the work."

Application Specifics: Most selected new plays are written by artists known to CATF; work is often commissioned. Four shows are selected per festival.

Fees: Not applicable.

Selection Criteria: "I choose new work based on my gut reaction," says Herendeen. "I am seeing plays that are relevant, immediate, and present. I am interested in contemporary works that examine contemporary issues."

Payments/Profits/Benefits: Confidentially arranged between artist and company.

Physical Production Details: The festival was founded in conjunction with Shepherd College. Spaces there encompass the Frank Arts Center (a 430-seat house) and the Studio Theater (a 130-seat house). "Rehearsals are done in the same rotating schedule as the shows will be performed by, with each show rehearsing once a day," says Herendeen. "The rehearsal period is four weeks, and we follow Equity repertory rules."

Housing: Provided for all company members.

Past Artists/Productions of Note: An illustrious list, including *The Late Henry Moss* by Sam Shepard; *Welcome to the Moon* by John Patrick Shanley; *Tough Choices for the New Century* by Jane Anderson; *Spike Heels* by Theresa Rebeck; plus numerous works by Joyce Carol Oates, Stephen Belber, Craig Wright, Richard Dresser, and many others.

Festival Flavor: This festival strives to enlighten audiences with intensely intelligent work, but it's not always completely serious—Richard Dresser's 1997 comedy *Below the Belt* was a big box-office hit.

The Bottom Line: Don't send off blind submissions here—you'd just be wasting your time. Instead, build your career, stay familiar with the work CATF is presenting, and work your way toward making a good impression on this fest's personnel.

Downtown Urban Theater Festival

Founded: 2002

Contact Info: c/o Abrons Arts Center, 466 Grand Street, New York, NY 10002. It's advised that you write to this fest in care of the above address, or contact publicist Marc Newell at (212) 807-1337 ext. 14 for information, as e-mail and Web site were unavailable at press time.

Performance Dates: Annually for about two weeks in May.

The Festival's Mission: This fest was established in the months following 9/11 to help pull Manhattan's downtown theater scene out of its artistic and financial doldrums. Dedicating itself subsequently to the needs of the urban playwright, the fest strives to provide a forum for original voices.

Application Specifics: Artistic director Reg E. Gaines (*Bring in 'Da Noise, Bring in 'Da Funk*) has resolved to give playwrights the chance to totally control their work within the festival environment. Blocking, direction, casting, and rehearsals all fully involve the writer. Your best bet is to contact the fest with an introduction letter and resume, before sending a writing sample.

Fees: Not applicable.

Selection Criteria: One play from an overseas writer is chosen annually; otherwise an average of six full-length plays and six one-acts are selected for production. A musical is also chosen.

Payments/Profits/Benefits: Three cash prizes of varying amounts are awarded for the productions chosen as Best Play, Best Short, and Audience Choice. The fest will also endeavor to develop these pieces further.

Physical Production Details: All productions are staged in the Abron Arts Center's Harry de Jur Playhouse and Recital Hall.

Housing: Many participants are locals; inquire as to arrangements
if you're a selected participant from out of town.

Past Artists/Productions of Note: *The Northern Kingdom* by
Nancy Fales Garrett.

Festival Flavor: This fest is overseen by an extremely distinguished advisory committee, members of which include
George C. Wolfe and Joie Lee. The event has proved itself
to be extremely popular and well-regarded among hip intellectual theatergoers, and has enjoyed big box office since
its debut.

The Bottom Line: Not only prestigious, but a slice of heaven
for playwrights who want the chance to freely express
themselves.

Ensemble Studio Theatre's One-Act Marathon

Founded (as a theatrical entity): 1972

Contact Info: Literary Department, Ensemble Studio Theatre,
549 West 52nd Street, New York, NY 10019
(212) 247-4982 (phone); (212) 664-0041 (fax)

E-mail: postmaster@ensemblestudiotheatre.org

Web site: *www.ensemblestudiotheatre.org*

Performance Dates: Annually in May-June.

The Festival's Mission: This world-renowned fest is guided by
E.S.T.'s literary principles: "originality, artistic merit, skill,
technique, and the potential for growth."

Application Specifics: All genres considered; plays must be not
shorter than ten minutes in performance length and no
longer than forty-five minutes. Submit your full script (typed
in standard format) with your name, address, and phone
number on the title page. A self-addressed, stamped
envelope has to be included if you'd like a response (or for
your script to be returned).

Fees: None.

Selection Criteria: Despite the obvious fact that E.S.T.'s prestigious company members encompass the highest caliber of theater artists in the world, and that many of their associated playwrights are invited to submit year-round, the company is admirably democratic in evaluating and accepting work from newcomers. Out of 2,000 or so scripts submitted each year, over 300 works are produced in total at E.S.T. every year (many from emerging writers); for the One-Act Marathon, 100 finalists are chosen, then 12 plays are produced from that number for the fest itself. E.S.T.'s lit department is also unusually generous in providing helpful feedback to playwrights about the quality of submitted scripts, whether a script is chosen or not. In a nutshell: send them your best stuff, and listen carefully to the evaluation you receive—it's going to be very perceptive.

Payments/Profits/Benefits: A full production in the Marathon, plus the play is published in the festival's annual anthology.

Physical Production Details: Leave all the details in E.S.T.'s incredibly competent hands. Your show will happen on the company's mainstage, be cast from its talent pool, and be teched completely in-house.

Housing: If chosen, inquire about availability.

Past Artists/Productions of Note: Founding Artistic Director Curt Dempster has given opportunities to scores of future Oscar, Emmy, Tony, Pulitzer Prize, and OBIE winners. Lauded writers such as Eduardo Machado were discovered by E.S.T.

Festival Flavor: The atmosphere at E.S.T. is both relaxed and heady. The theater's highly efficient staff is very artist-friendly and welcoming, and you'll feel at home instantly—but hey, that attractive girl running lines over in the corner just might be Cynthia Nixon. Go in knowing you'll see very famous faces, then forget about it and act like a pro.

The Bottom Line: A must-try for playwrights who know they're working to their full potential.

The Genesius Guild Events

Founded: 1994

Contact Info: Thomas Morrissey, Artistic Director, the Genesius Guild, 520 Eighth Avenue, 3rd Floor—Suite 329, New York, NY 10018-6507

(212) 244-5404 (phone); (212) 591-6503 (fax)

E-mail: Tom@GenesiusGuild.org

Web site: *www.GenesiusGuild.org*

Performance Dates: See Web site for up-to-date information.

The Festival's Mission: The Genesius Guild's value is more than just a single fest it offers (although it does indeed sponsor performance events such evenings of comic one-acts, staged readings, and a cabaret performance series). Why it's included here is simple: its dedication to the creation of new plays and musicals. In the words of Tom Morrissey, artistic director, "The name is after Saint Genesius, who was the patron saint of actors, but I always immediately have to say after that that no way are we any kind of a religious organization—far from it! The basis of the company is creating and developing new work. What we try to do is develop as many different types of programming as possible that artists can get involved in, so that we can look and see, What is it that creates new work? How is new work created? How do you create a new aesthetic in theater? I also look at how we model our company a little bit the way Joe Papp worked. If you look at Joe Papp's theater, *A Chorus Line* did come out of that theater. He also did *Hair, For Colored Girls* . . . David Rabe was one of his playwrights; Mabou Mines was supported by the Public Theater for fourteen years—it's quite a diverse group of people. What he used to do was identify and find artists he liked, and whose work he thought was good, and rather than work with them on whatever project interested him when he discovered them, he'd usually ask them, 'What's next for you? What do you want to work on next?' And that's what our program is geared towards doing."

Application Specifics: Send a script, or mail your resume with a synopsis, treatment or proposal. Then go to the Guild, familiarize yourself with the kind of work that's currently being presented, and introduce yourself to Tom (who is a lovely guy) or any other Guild member. Talk about your work.

Fees: Not applicable.

Selection Criteria: "We have a group called our Script Club," says Morrissey. It's made up approximately of thirty to forty actors, writers, and directors and other theater professionals, all volunteers. They meet twice a month, and when they meet, they're given out scripts that we receive as submissions. They take those scripts, they read them, they take them back to the following meeting two weeks later, and they discuss the scripts that they read. Everyone gets to hear what everybody else is saying about the different scripts, and then they're passed out again. Each script is read by a minimum of two readers, sometimes up to four or six readers. We purposefully try to pull into this group as many diverse theater artists a possible, to get different viewpoints. The whole purpose of it is hopefully to have pieces that are exciting and interesting, that one person may like, another person may not like. I think one of the things that makes our company both difficult and different is, we don't have a filter that pieces come through that they must fit into." Scripts deemed interesting go on to a committee, which is headed up by the different programs run by the Guild (a directors' program, actors' lab, and writing groups), so pieces can be picked out to be worked on.

Payments/Profits/Benefits: The Guild makes efforts to introduce playwrights to commercial producers. "Normally what we do is take a percentage—usually it's 1 to 2 percent—as a developmental fee," says Morrissey. "It comes from the commercial producers when they take (a piece) up." Pieces that look as though they might have future potential are categorized as "target projects" and are given as many resources as possible to flourish.

Physical Production Details: Inquire about specifics as they affect a chosen project.

Housing: Not applicable.

Past Artists/Productions of Note: *Box* by Fred Shahadi; *Last Sunday in June* by John Tolan.

Festival Flavor: "Normally when we do anything that's termed a 'festival,' it's because we're looking for a specific thing," says Morrissey. "It's really geared toward outreach. You know, you can judge people's work a lot of times by going to see pieces that they've done, and you can also judge their work a lot by what's written on the paper, but until you actually work together with someone, you don't really know. So it gives us an opportunity to do that."

The Bottom Line: A great company where talented artists can collaborate for years to come.

Humana Festival of New American Plays (Actors Theatre of Louisville)

Founded: 1979

Contact Info: New Play Program, Attn: Amy Wegener, Actors Theatre of Louisville, 316 West Main Street, Louisville, Kentucky 40202-4218

(502) 584-1265 (phone); (502) 561-3306 (fax)

Web site: *www.actorstheatre.org/humana*

Performance Dates: Annually each February/March.

The Festival's Mission: Artistic manager Zan Sawyer-Dailey stresses the fact that the playwrights' needs and wants drive this fest, above everything else: "The very first thing that we ask each playwright as we settle that we're going to be presenting their piece is, 'Who do you like to direct?' The playwrights in our festival have a very great voice. This is the playwrights' festival, and it's our main concern."

Application Specifics: Full-length and one-act scripts are accepted only through a literary agent or with a letter of recommendation from the artistic director or lit manager of a professional theater or playwrights' organization. If you don't have these kinds of connections, though, don't despair: The festival will accept a letter expressing your interest along with a synopsis and ten-page script cutting. If they like what you present, festival personnel will contact you to see the whole script.

Fees: None.

Selection Criteria: "Any type of material is appropriate to submit to us, but we are interested in certain kinds of things," says Sawyer-Dailey. "Obviously, we're looking for unique, new voices, dealing in issues that are more of a topical nature. We've sort of read the romances—it's not that we don't like romances, but if they're going to be that, we want them presented in some sort of a unique fashion. We're obviously very interested in nurturing new and emerging talent. We are also interested in anchoring the festival sometimes with a more well-known, more populist type of playwright. We are always interested in diversity—sexual diversity, multi-cultural diversity, international diversity. Those are a few of the things we really look at. We try—we're not always successful—we try to weight the balance of gender. It's kind of interesting; this year, I think, all but one of the playwrights are women, and all but one of the directors are men. You just sort of try your best to equal it out."

Payments/Profits/Benefits: Inquire about guidelines if chosen.

Physical Production Details: Handled completely by ATL tech staff.

Housing: Inquire about availability if chosen.

Past Artists/Productions of Note: Highly esteemed works include *The Gin Game* by D.L. Coburn, *Crimes of the Heart* by Beth Henley, *Dinner with Friends* by Donald Margulies, *Keely and Du* by Jane Martin, *Slavs!* by Tony Kushner, *2* by Romulus Linney, *Polaroid Stories* by Naomi Iizuka, *Sans-culottes in the Promised Land* by Kirsten Greenidge, and many, many more.

Festival Flavor: Sawyer-Dailey explains, "As an organization, we probably use dramaturgy more throughout our entire season—we have a dramaturg on every production. And our staff—well, they're quite incredible, but they are also very perceptive and very willing. Their function is to sort of ask the hard questions, and to keep the director and the playwright trying to move forward in terms of solving the thematic issues, making sure, 'Is this what you really want? This is what's coming across.' To that end, they get very, very involved in the rewrite process. Our function is to try to help navigate it, and then of course, there's always a certain amount of negotiation."

The Bottom Line: Peerless in terms of prestige and artistic merit.

The John F. Kennedy Center for the Performing Arts' New Visions/New Voices

Founded: 1991

Contact Info: Deidre Kelly Lavrakas/Kim Peter Kovac, New Visions/New Voices, The Kennedy Center, Education Department, P.O. Box 10808, Arlington, VA 22210 (202) 416-8880 (phone); (202) 416-8297 (fax)

E-mail: yfp@kennedy-center.org

Web site: *www.kennedycenter.com*

Performance Dates: This residency program takes place for one week every other May in even-numbered years. Focused solely on new works for young audiences and families, artistic teams collaborate intensively for five days rehearsing works in development, then present their projects as staged readings to a professional audience (consisting of artists, academic, and administrators). Monitored feedback is given through a discussion after each performance.

The Festival's Mission: Encouraging the creation of the best-quality new plays and musicals for young people, while giving artists a wide berth creatively (work can be submitted for consideration at any stage of its genesis, from treatment to production-ready draft). It helps that Kim Peter Kovac and Deidre Kelly Lavarkas, who run New Visions/New Voices together, are both artists themselves. "One of the happy accidents is that Deidre and I were both directors in the first New Visions—I for a play commissioned by Birmingham Children's Theater, Deidre for a Kennedy Center piece," explains Kovac. "I think that helped us come to a visceral understanding of the needs of the artist, and, as we work from the outside, keep a focus on that."

Application Specifics: Material submitted must be part of an upcoming season at a theater. That theater should submit a full proposal including a director and playwright, plus the material in its current form.

Fees: Not applicable.

Selection Criteria: "The adjudication is two-part," says Kovac. "First of all, all the projects are read by two or three outside readers. The top-ranked projects are then read by a Kennedy Center committee (I typically read them all). The projects are 'blinded,' as it were—with the name of the writer and theater removed, so the adjudicators are reading based on the quality of the work, not the name of the writer or theater. Information about who submitted the work is only revealed at the very end of the adjudication process. The most important factor is the quality of the proposed project. Other factors are in the mix: diversity in all forms—cultural, geographic, size of theater. We try to find a mix of shows for the festival as a whole—plays for different age groups, a mix of musicals and non-musicals, etc. Sometimes the Kennedy Center chooses to workshop some of its own pieces in development."

Payment/Profits/Benefits: Selected theater personnel receive an honorarium plus travel expenses.

Physical Production Details: New Visions/New Voices goes up in the Kennedy Center's Theater Lab space in Washington, D.C. Three to five hours a day of Equity-stipulated rehearsals take place for five days leading up to performance (Equity actors are cast by the Kennedy Center in each piece). Tech support and personnel (SMs, dramaturgs, musical directors) are supplied by the Kennedy Center.

Housing: Each theater is responsible for covering its personnel.

Past Artists/Productions of Note: Recent companies participating in the festival include Honolulu Theatre for Youth, Omaha Theater Company for Young People, Blue Shift Theatre Ensemble/Actor's Company of Pennsylvania, Oregon Children's Theatre, Seattle Children's Theatre, and Childsplay.

Festival Flavor: "I think the greatest achievement is the accumulation of wonderful playwrights, composers, directors, and theaters that have worked at New Visions," says Kovac. "There's a unique energy to the fact that it's this playwright and this director who will doing this script next season. We at the Kennedy Center work very hard to say to the artistic teams that we have no agenda other than that their piece move to the next stage of its development. That's one of the program's strengths—we really view it as a service to the field. Another very strong statement the program makes is in its diversity of casting. The program is constructed so that we of the Kennedy Center do the casting of the shows. Deidre speaks with the directors, knows the local acting pool, and casts the shows. We have strong actors in Washington, and we believe very strongly in non-traditional casting in all its forms. Since it's about process, not product, actors who can get the right interpretation and spirit are cast, not necessarily the ones who would normally be cast. Last New Visions, the Baby Jesus in a musical version of *The Selfish Giant* was played by an African-American woman and Henry in *The Red Badge of Courage* was played by a forty-something man, not the teenager that the character is."

The Bottom Line: An esteemed and enriching opportunity to collaborate with the best.

Moving Arts Premiere One-Act Competition/Festival

Founded: 1995

Contact Info: Trey Nichols, Literary Director, Moving Arts, Premiere One-Act Competition, Los Angeles Theatre Center, 514 S. Spring Street, Los Angeles, CA 90013 (213) 622-8906 (phone), (213) 622-8946 (fax)

E-mail: treynichols@movingarts.org, info@movingarts.org

Web site: *www.movingarts.org*

Performance Dates: Two alternating programs of one-acts presented over eight weeks each autumn.

The Festival's Mission: The fest's official mission statement stresses a desire to present "original drama or comedy that is bold, challenging, and edgy; plays with complex characters, evocative language, strong relationships, and evocative themes that speak to the human condition in a fresh or startling way. We are not limited to any particular style or genre; we are confined only by the inherent truth of the material, so long as the emphasis is on the theatrical." And, in the words of Trey Nichols: "To keep the one-act play alive as an important dramatic literary genre; to bring attention and acclaim to good writing; to build and reinforce relationships with playwrights; to put on a kick-ass festival of plays, and hang out with a great group of people; to get the work out there in the world."

Application Specifics: Check Web site for most current application specifics. Appropriate length for submissions is super-flexible (from five to sixty pages). Submissions do not have to be world premieres, but must be Los Angeles–area premiere material.

Fees: A small $10 entrance fee.

Selection Criteria: All genres/subjects considered. The dues-paying membership of Moving Arts (actors, writers, and directors) judges one-acts submitted to the competition. The process works like this: A team of core readers reads every script submitted twice (or three times, if a tie-breaking opinion is required) before sending chosen scripts to the next round of competition. A 1-to-5 scoring system categorizes entries. Plays with the highest scores move to the "frozen reading" phase, a set of closed-door sessions in which the material is read aloud and evaluated by company members and invited associates. Each play is then debated, and a list of finalists is then chosen. (The final word rests with the theatre's artistic director and art council, however.)

FYI: Make sure your submission looks cosmetically perfect if you want to impress these folks. "Formatting and neatness, a brief professional cover letter—essentially author hygiene—are very important, like making a first impression at a job interview," stresses Nichols. "Would you hire a manicurist with dirty fingernails?"

Payments/Profits/Benefits: A $200 cash prize, plus all production costs covered and a full Festival production. Additionally, all festival playwrights receive a percentage of box-office revenue. Industry folk regularly check out this fest, and do indeed pick up work. (*The Scream* by DT Archer was recently optioned by Tori Spelling, for example.)

Physical Production Details: The festival space is a fifty-seat black box with a modified thrust stage (diamond-shaped, with audience seating on either side), located on the fifth floor of the Los Angeles Theater Center. Full sound (CD and MiniDisc player) and mic capabilities as needed are available, plus modest but sufficient pro lighting instruments. It's best to keep tech needs flexible. Actors are expected to pitch in for set changes, as well. Tech is held in the mainstage space usually a week prior to the festival going up.

Housing: Not provided, but Moving Arts is happy to offer suggestions for lodging if asked.

Past Artists/Productions of Note: *Busted Jesus Comix* by David Johnston, which was brought back for a second run at Moving Arts due to popular demand; *The Body of Bourne* by John Belluso, which was subsequently produced at the Mark Taper Forum; *War Music* by Bryan Davidson, which enjoyed further success at both the Playwright's Arena and the Geffen Playhouse.

Festival Flavor: "It can get a little crazy, but I'm happy to report that no fistfights have broken out during any of our festivals yet," jokes Nichols. "Our backstage is tiny, separated from the backs of the audience's heads by only a wooden board, so every movement, whisper, or costume change is audible." Despite the cramped quarters, Nichols reports good artist camaraderie. "Generally, the actors get along well—they're in the show together, most are company members, many are friends outside the festival."

The Bottom Line: Despite the company culture, definitely a welcoming place for playwrights. Opportunities abound here to get your work noticed.

National Audio Theatre Festivals

Founded: 1979

Contact Info: Sue Zizza, Executive Director, National Audio Theatre Festivals, 115 Dikeman Street, Hampstead, NY 11150 (516) 483-8321 (phone); (516) 583-7583

Web site: *www.natf.org*

Performance Dates: A week-long conference, the Audio Theatre Workshop, is held annually in June.

The Festival's Mission: To encourage writers of radio plays, and encourage artists within the industry to learn artistically and technically; to encourage the use of the art form in all media. Sue Zizza, the organization's executive director, says of the conference, "At the end of the week, we put on a live show, so that everybody gets to see how all these things we've been telling them about throughout the week really are integrated. Now, our goal is to encourage them to go home and do studio work more than live work. Because unless you've got a really high-quality crew there, it's hard to produce very high-quality live work. But it's not impossible. The other thing is, a lot of these artists like to go back home to their amateur theater community and begin by producing live shows, because it's not as expensive; it's much more accessible. So we try to give them the basic skills that they need to be able to create art in their own community, whether that's in a live venue or a studio venue."

Application Specifics: NATF sponsors the Audio Drama Script Competition, winning selections of which are produced during NATF's Live Performance Workshop. Scripts should be original and about twenty-five minutes long; strong female characters, multi-cultural casting opportunities, and diverse issues are desired. Two to four winners have been chosen historically. Check out the latest up-to-date competition information on the Web site.

Fees: The Audio Drama Script Competition charges a $25 entry fee; to participate in the workshop week, the cost is between $375 and $425 per participant.

Selection Criteria: Zizza says, "They have to use the media in its best way. Unfortunately, sometimes what happens with our script competition is that we get stage plays that have not really been considered for the audio-only medium. The things that we look for—the average radio station or broadcast outlet still pretty much only wants to deal with a half-hour format. Occasionally, if it's a holiday or something like that, they'll go to an hour. But for the most part, if a station is going to pick something up, it needs to be in a half-hour format, or it needs to be in a modular format—little five-minute bites so that stations can run it in and around the news, or they'll cut away from 'All Things Considered,' or whatever. So we try to ask playwrights to keep their work to about a half-hour—within the twenty-six- to twenty-eight-minute range, and that's also just to make it more possible to mount two or three plays throughout the workshop week, and not just do one. That gives more acting possibilities to our workshop participants. Additionally, we want pieces that have strong characters in them. You know, you've only got a half an hour—you've really got to create something here that's gonna give you good, strong character development right from the top. That's character-driven—that's not necessarily event-driven or plot-driven. You have to meet these people in the first thirty seconds, get to know who they are, and see and hear them in your mind's eye."

Payments/Profits/Benefits: $800 split between the winning writers of the Audio Drama Script Competition, plus free workshop participation. All rights retained by authors except for initial production in the Live Performance Workshop. Script winners are placed in a book and made available (for three years) to producers who might be interested in them; producers contact authors directly. "We really are looking to create a body of scripts that would allow new producers, mid-level producers, an opportunity to have something to work with that is of reasonable quality."

Physical Production Details: The Audio Theatre Workshop is held on the campus of Southwest Missouri State University.

Housing: Available for a fee—either shared accommodations in a dorm (about $120) or at a local hotel (about $315).

Past Artists/Productions of Note: Broadway star Jim Dale is just one of the many distinguished artists who has contributed his wisdom to the workshop week.

Festival Flavor: This is a very professional environment, and should be approached as such.

The Bottom Line: No one is more informed or experienced in the field of radio drama than Sue Zizza. If this is a writing genre you want to pursue, she's your mentor.

NAMT—National Alliance for Musical Theatre Festival of New Musicals

Founded: 1989

Contact Info: Daniella Topol, New Works Program Director, National Alliance for Musical Theatre, 520 Eighth Avenue, Suite 301, 3rd Floor, New York, NY 10018
(212) 714-6668 (phone); (212) 714-0469 (fax)

E-mail: info@namt.net

Web site: *www.namt.net*

Performance Dates: Contact for details.

The Festival's Mission: To introduce noteworthy theater producers to composers/writers of new musicals from all over the world; to nurture new work and collaboration; to encourage diversity and future production. According to Daniella Topol, the program's director, "NAMT (the producing organization) started very informally—it was just a bunch of friends who were running theaters around the country who wanted to get together and talk to each other. And that was also what the festival was about in the beginning—because there were a lot of producers doing new work on their stages around the country, but unless you were traveling all over the country, you couldn't see the work. So they thought, Why don't we create a festival in New York of the work we're doing around the country? So its original purpose was to showcase the work that our members were producing around the country in New York for one another. And then it gradually expanded, and it became, Well, here's a great opportunity to actually shop for new work. And it's not necessarily new work that we've done yet, but it could be new work that we want to do. And so it's a combination now of people who want to showcase work that they've done, and people who want to shop for new work, and for that reason, we've opened it up to non-members to submit to the festival. Some great partnerships have formed between members and non-members through the festival."

Application Specifics: Up-to-date information is available at the Web site address above. In general, submission requirements are stiff—your work must be submitted by a NAMT member organization, an NAMT Alumni Festival writer, or a non-member professional theater that's been in business for two years or longer and has a minimum operating budget of $50,000. If you qualify, you must submit an application form; a bio; copyright proof; a letter of recommendation from your submitting organization; four copies of your script with author(s)'s names listed on only one copy; a one-hundred-word max synopsis and character breakdown in each script; four copies of your score on CD, sequenced to the script; and a self-addressed, stamped postcard for confirmation that your package has been received by the festival.

Fees: A $35 administration fee.

Selection Criteria: "The reason why we're so careful about who can submit is because the people reading the scripts are artistic directors of NAMT member theaters. We don't have any sort of reading committee of volunteers. We don't have any kind of ad hoc interim vetting situation. It really is the people running the theaters who are reading the work, and so it's very important that there are the filters in place to make sure the work that's being submitted is really ready," explains Topol. "'Ready' is such a complicated issue. It's like, when are the cookies done? Everybody has different taste, and you just want to eat them! You've been working on your project so damn long, and you've had two readings and that kind of situation, and you're just . . . you're ready! What we've found is, the work that's been through considerable development and/or previous productions, as long as they're not first-class commercial productions, are eligible for our festival. We encourage the work to have had a workout before it gets to us because our festival is so public. People have one shot—you have one shot to impress people, and that's it. We've seen work that has not been ready, been in the festival, and that can kill a show. Or what also happens because we just do the presentations as forty-five-minute excerpts, is that producers get wowed by the forty-five minutes and they want the rest, and the material isn't there. That doesn't mean that the shows that are done in the festival won't have more work done on them—they always will. We're encouraging those works that have had some relationship to a professional theater or producer to be submitted to our festival because we know that if you have no professional theater somehow connected to your piece yet, then your piece probably isn't ready."

Payments/Profits/Benefits: For quality material, the sky can be the limit. "Peter Marx from the *New York Times* called the festival 'the marketplace for new musicals,'" says Topol. "People are shopping for work. There are a lot of producers who can use their imaginations and fill in the blanks that aren't there, and there are a lot that can't. In any case, you're up against other works that don't have the blanks. You've got to put your best foot forward."

Physical Production Details: Traditionally held at the John Houseman and Douglas Fairbanks Off-Broadway theaters on Manhattan's 42nd Street Theatre Row. "Every piece rehearses for twenty-nine hours, including performance time," says Topol. "They do not usually get a chance to rehearse in the theaters, because we're doing the festival in spaces where they have shows running. The goal is to keep the presentations as simple as possible: It's chairs, it's music stands, it's stools." Amplification is provided; tracks can be used in addition to piano.

Housing: Inquire about availability if selected.

Past Artists/Productions of Note: *Thoroughly Modern Millie*, by Richard Morris, Dick Scanlan, and Jeanine Tesori; *Summer of '42* by Hunter Foster and David Kirshenbaum; *Sarah, Plain and Tall* by Julia Jordan, Neil Benjamin, and Lawrence O'Keefe; *Harold & Maude: The Musical* by Tom Jones and Joseph Thalken, based on the film by Colin Higgins.

Festival Flavor: "The vibe is good—mostly curious and excited," relates Topol. "Often you see most of the writers and some of the cast members attending the other shows. We really try to program a cross-section of types of pieces. It's not like we're trying to fill a particular slot—like, we have to have the family show. We actually have the freedom to respond to whatever it is that comes through the submissions process. But it is a cross-section, so they're not really competing against each other. In fact, if a couple of shows are good, that just makes the buzz about the festival stronger, and people will stay longer in the day. It's in everybody's best interest for the other shows to go well."

The Bottom Line: Ultra-competitive, but absolutely invaluable.

New Perspectives Theatre Company's Voices from the Edge Festival

Founded: 1998

Contact Info: New Perspectives Theatre Company, Voices From the Edge, 750 8th Avenue, Room 601, New York, NY 10036 (212) 730-2030 (phone)

E-mail: vfte@newperspectivestheatre.org

Web site: *www.newperspectivestheatre.org*

Performance Dates: Two-weeks biennially each February.

The Festival's Mission: According to New Perspectives Theatre founder and artistic director Melody Brooks, Voices from the Edge brings the work of artists performing at the grassroots level to the attention of the larger public. "In 1997, we met a number of talented African-American artists through a small arts-in-education organization," she recalls. "These writers and performers were creating extraordinary work, much of it based on their personal experiences in helping populations in need—youth offenders, the homeless, female prisoners, persons with HIV/AIDS, public school children, etc.—through workshops and developmental programs." New Perspectives Theatre created the fest in order to give these artists an important forum for their plays, solo pieces, storytelling, poetry, and multimedia work. "Some of it is raw, some more polished, but it all fulfilled our vision of what theater is about: to educate and enlighten as well as entertain; to move audiences on a visceral level and challenge them to become agents for change."

Application Specifics: E-mail a synopsis of your project with your playwright's bio and a production history to the above address. (If there's interest, you'll be asked to mail the complete script.) Visit Web site for most up-to-date guidelines and specifics.

Fees: None.

Selection Criteria: "We have a team of people who read the submissions and then share their opinions with each other," says Brooks. "There are no instant turn-offs (other than poorly written scripts), but we tend to look for 1) quality, 2) originality, and 3) a collection of work that showcases the diversity of the themes and writing styles emerging from the African-American community." Artists who are well regarded by the company are sometimes invited to participate, or if they have made a good impression at the fest, invited back in the future.

Payments/Profits/Benefits: New Perspectives has taken a number of festival offerings to the next level of production. "Some have received additional staged readings in subsequent festivals; some have been workshopped and received a limited-run production; and others have been produced under the Equity showcase code," explains Brooks.

Physical Production Details: A Manhattan seventy-seat black box—both the seating and staging areas are quite flexible and measure twenty feet by roughly fifty feet. A general lighting plot, sound equipment, and standard props are provided.

Housing: Not provided, but the theater is glad to offer inexpensive lodging/dining suggestions.

Past Artists/Productions of Note: Many talented actors have worked here, including Ted Lange (who starred as Isaac on TV's *The Love Boat*), OBIE-winner Stephanie Barry, and Novella Nelson. Lange wrote and performed the fest fave *Lemon Meringue Parade*; other noteworthy plays have included *Good People* by L. Trey Wilson and *Unrequited Love* by Melissa Maxwell.

Festival Flavor: A sense of community is strongly cultivated. "This (the vibe itself) is something we have worked very hard to create, to get people to understand that they are participating in something more than just their own presentation," says Brooks. To this end, festival artists are encouraged to (and do) see and support other festival presentations.

The Bottom Line: A wonderful place for the socially conscious artist to get out his message.

The Playwrights' Center Playlabs Festival

Founded: circa 1980 (Center founded in 1971)

Contact Info: Kristin Gandrow, director of new play development, The Playwrights' Center, 2301 Franklin Ave., East, Minneapolis, MN 55406
(612) 332-7481 (phone); (612) 332-6037 (fax)

E-mail: pwcenter@mtn.org

Web site: *www.pwcenter.org*

Performance Dates: Two weeks annually. Check Web site for
most current upcoming dates.

The Festival's Mission: "To provide a diverse group of exciting
playwrights and plays a two-week collaboration workshop
and the necessary resources to develop their plays to a point
where the work can be presented in a public performance
reading," says Gandrow. Some projects are done via collaboration with other companies (like the Guthrie and Children's Theatre Company), who pay to put a playwright they
select into the program (which covers the direct costs
of wages paid to Playlabs artists). Gandrow adds, "Our
strengths are dramaturgical and text-based, as well as having
strong actors. We pride ourselves in hiring excellent and
appropriate directors and dramaturgs—sometimes selected
by the playwright; sometimes I'm the matchmaker for the
creative team."

Application Specifics: There are several ways playwrights can get
work considered: 1) Several slots are filled via the theater's
full national competition; 2) a winner may be included
from the McKnight Residency and Commission Fellowship
competition (a highly selective contest for nationally significant playwrights outside Minnesota); 3) by having work on
slate for production during the theater's regular season;
4) or through hookup via the Guthrie or another sponsoring
theater. Contact theater or check Web site for most
current specifics.

Fees: There's a $15 application fee if you're not part of the
Playwrights' Center membership.

Selection Criteria: Gandrow cites the following points: "Strength
of playwright and play (artistry, creativity, high level of craft,
diversity of play's aesthetic style and also of playwright);
playwright's stated goals are focused and achievable in a
two-week workshop; must be new plays, not submitted to
Playlabs before." What she doesn't want to see: "Revisions to

a previous submission that the writer insists make the play wholly new (except that the title, characters, issues, theme are still the same!)."

Payments/Profits/Benefits: A per diem. Plus, Gandrow says, "Most promising plays get sent out to theaters around the U.S. Many regional theaters' lit managers request all or some of each year's festival plays because they know and expect the caliber of the work from us to be high."

Physical Production Details: A 120-seat flexible black box; stage has a rough estimate measurement of 24 feet wide by 24 feet deep. Limited sound, light, and tech allowed; few or no props. Artists are urged to focus on text development, not stagecraft, so chairs and music stands or a table generally make up a set. Three to four rehearsal hours and a three hour tech in space allotted per presentation.

Housing: Fully provided, plus breakfast, transportation, airport transfers, and rides into town for artists coming from outside the Twin Cities. Theater guests also are given group rates and transportation from a hotel, plus breakfast and a couple of evening meals.

Past Artists/Productions of Note: Tons of terrific playwrights have taken part, including Marion McClinton, Honour Kane, Carson Becker, Lee Blessing, Chay Yew, Luis Alfaro, Bridget Carpenter, Jeffrey Hatcher, Laurie Carlos, Melanie Marnich, Carlyle Brown, Craig Wright, Lisa D'Amour, Erik Ehn, Naomi Iiuka, Neena Barber, Diana Son, Carson Kreitzer, W. David Hancock, and Caridad Svich.

Festival Flavor: "There's an incredibly fun, colorful exciting atmosphere here in the Center," enthuses Gandrow. It's a very social scene among its seventy-five participants and the theater artists who attend from all over the country, with lots of chances to network and a big dinner held on the final night of the fest.

The Bottom Line: One of the country's most prestigious developmental events.

The Rhinoceros Theater Festival (The Curious Theatre Branch)

Founded: 1988

Contact Info: Jenny Magnus, Beau O'Reilly, co-founders, The Rhinoceros Theater Festival, 7001 N. Glenwood, Chicago, Illinois
(773) 274-6660 (phone)

Web site: *www.rhinocerostheaterfestival.com*

Performance Dates: Annually, usually during four days toward the end of October.

The Festival's Mission: In the words of Jenny Magnus, "The overall mission of the Rhino Fest is to produce new work. Whatever that might mean to someone." Originally part of the Bucktown Fine Arts Festival, this fest showcases theater, music, and performance pieces from Chicago's experimental scene. Magnus and O'Reilly were members of a cabaret rock-and-roll band, and wanted to use their creative impulse to spotlight the new work of others from the community. "There was no model of any kind at the beginning, other than to get a lot of work together within the same organized context, whether it be geographical or ideological or temporal," she explains.

Application Specifics: Contact the festival for current specifics, which vary. "Our criteria change from year to year. Sometimes it is literally that a friend has something new and wants to produce it," says Magnus. "Sometimes it is a student of one of us (Magnus teaches at Columbia College) who wants to make the leap from academia to the real world. We have, in past years, invited submissions, read scripts, and made decisions of inclusion based on nothing more scientific than taste."

Fees: No festival admission fees or upfront fees of any kind for festival artists. The Curious Theatre Branch takes a percentage of the door for the venue, and a percentage for the festival.

Selection Criteria: "I guess the top three criteria would be originality, length (we do two shows a night, mostly) and set complexity. How well something will fit into a festival context is uppermost in our minds," says Magnus. "I don't think there are any automatic turn-offs, other than something being really poorly written and stupid."

Payments/Profits/Benefits: Companies average a 40 percent door profit.

Physical Production Details: The festival was produced for many years in storefronts, but now has a permanent home in the Curious Theatre Branch's new North Glenwood space. "The space seats between forty-nine and seventy and is a concrete floor with risered seats," elaborates Magnus. "We have a forty-channel board and about thirty lights, and a stereo speaker sound system with a multiple-CD player." Four or more in-space rehearsals are allowed.

Housing: "Housing has been provided on rare occasions in the past," says Magnus. "We had touring companies from Cleveland and Germany a few different times, and found places for them to stay. Usually someone coming from out of town has a personal connection, and they make their own arrangements. If there is a possibility for reciprocation, i.e., a company from somewhere that wants to sponsor Curious to come there, we would make housing arrangements in exchange for being sponsored when we went to their hometown."

Past Artists/Productions of Note: Theater for the Age of Gold's *The Problematic Cartoonist*; Theater Oobleck's *The Hunchback Variations* and *Babette's Feast*; the Curious Theatre Branch's *Illustrious Bloodspill* and *Eddie: A Man in his Skin*; work by playwrights Michael Smith and Sue Cargill.

Festival Flavor: "The Rhino has been described as a living Web site," says Magnus. "The connectibility, community feeling, sharing of stuff, seeing everything that's playing, and general summer camp quality really comes over anyone who is around in August, September, and October. We call it Rhino Bliss and it's one of the things that keeps us interested in killing ourselves every year for other people's work. There are usually a lot of people hanging around the spaces, and a frantic rush between shows to get one show out and another one in, and a lot of tension sometimes, but a wonderful feeling of something happening."

The Bottom Line: If artistic integrity is more important than commercial cash-in to you, and you do quality work that's audacious, you'll find a great home here.

Short Attention Span PlayFEST

Founded: 1999

Contact Info: Kimberly Davis Basso, Artistic Director, Atlantis Playmakers, c/o 4611 Monroe Street, Hollywood, Florida (954) 962-4534 (South Coast phone); (978) 667-0550 (East Coast phone)

E-mail: kdb@AtlantisPlaymakers.com

Web site: *www.atlantisplaymakers.com*

Performance Dates: Annually during the last ten days in June.

The Festival's Mission: To world-premiere high-quality, short new works.

Application Specifics: All genres considered. Scripts must be fifteen pages or under. Monologues (ten pages or under) are also accepted. Playwrights should note that a maximum of four actors will be cast per production, so any more characters than that should be able to be doubled. Send full script with a cover page containing all contact information. Scripts can be e-mailed to Kimberly Davis Basso at the above e-mail address, but only in Word format.

Fees: None.

Selection Criteria: This fest is pretty competitive, and draws the work of strong writers from all across the United States. The good news is that there's no set number of scripts that are selected for the festival, so if a bunch of great plays get submitted, a bunch of great plays can potentially be staged.

Payment/Profits/Benefits: An honorarium goes to all playwrights whose work is chosen to be part of the festival. In addition, all chosen work is eligible to be Best of Fest: Your production could score one of two Audience Awards, which come with $250 (the writer splits this with his/her director and cast). Atlantis only reserves the right to present each work's world premiere—after that, all rights revert to the playwright.

Physical Production Details: The festival itself is held not in Florida (where some Atlantis business is headquartered), but in Billerica, Massachusetts, at Dale Hall, 5 Andover Road. Minimum sets and tech allowed. (Show changes are lightning-fast, due to multiple performances per evening.) All festival directors are affiliated with the company.

Housing: Inquire about availability if selected.

Past Artists/Productions of Note: *The Entourage* by Daniel S. Basso; *Cookie Pusher* by Dian Russell; *Code Red* by Anne Hanley.

Festival Flavor: Very friendly, but fast-paced. Writers should work all the kinks out of their material before they arrive at the festival, and that means all necessary rewrites and read-throughs should happen on your own time and turf.

The Bottom Line: A super opportunity for writers looking to get some acclaim.

TheatreWorks New Works Festival

Founded: 2002

Contact Info: Kent Nicholson, Director of New Works, Theatre-Works New Works Festival, P.O. Box 50548, Palo Alto, CA 94303-0458
(650) 463-1960 (phone)

E-mail: Through theater Web site only.

Web site: *www.theatreworks.org*

Performance Dates: Annually each April-May for approximately five days.

The Festival's Mission: Part of TheatreWorks' developmental New Works Initiative, this fest provides composers and book writers of musicals the opportunity to collaborate on and present top-notch new productions.

Application Specifics: No unsolicited material. Work is accepted for consideration through agent submission. Other eligible work includes scripts produced Off-Off Broadway or regionally outside of the Bay Area, musicals not produced in the Bay Area in over five years, and undeveloped plays and musicals. Initial submissions should consist of a cover letter, a short synopsis, a ten-page cutting of dialogue, a production history, the writer's theatrical resume, a cassette containing the score, and a self-addressed, stamped package/envelope.

Fees: None.

Selection Criteria: Some of today's most gifted authors and composers have already participated in the fest and the New Works Initiative, including Tony and Pulitzer Prize winner Marsha Norman, Henry Krieger, Hunter Foster, Bill Russell, and many others. The bar is set high when it comes to getting a spot here.

Payments/Profits/Benefits: Once a piece is premiered and favorably received at the festival, it may receive a full Theatre-Works staging the subsequent season. Inquire about additional project-specific arrangements if chosen to participate.

Physical Production Details: The company's Mountain View Center for Performing Arts stage; the Lucie Stern Theatre space.

Past Productions/Artists of Note: Numerous, including *My Antonia* by Scott and Stephen Schwartz, which was developed at TheatreWorks, world-premiered at the fest, and moved on to a full regular season production (in addition to whipping up lots of press and audience enthusiasm).

Festival Flavor: Very supportive. Artists are encouraged at the company's winter writers' retreat, and given lots of invaluable feedback throughout their project's genesis. Shows are extremely well cast through alternative and multi-cultural talent pools. All in all, a very warm and humane creative vibe.

The Bottom Line: Composers and authors with a terrifically promising project and/or a superior resume should absolutely go for it.

Trustus Playwrights' Festival

Founded: 1988

Contact Info: Jon Tuttle, Literary Manager, Trustus Playwrights' Festival, Trustus Theatre, P.O. Box 11721, Columbia, SC 29211-1721
(803) 254-9732 (phone); (803) 771-9153 (fax)

E-mail: trustus@trustus.org

Web site: *www.trustus.org*

Performance Dates: This competition's winning play receives a staged reading before an audience each August, then is mounted as a full Trustus production the following August.

The Festival's Mission: "The shorthand goes like this: 'Trust us—we do good plays here,'" says Tuttle. "When they founded Trustus (as a theater) in 1985, Jim and Kay Thigpen were committed to doing contemporary, cutting-edge, and original plays—and at the same time to staying in business." Giving examples of non-festival, Trustus-produced material like *Proof*, *Gross Indecency*, *Spinning into Butter*, and *Jar in the Floor*, Tuttle elaborates, "If you recognize any of the titles above, you know what we're looking for: plays with strong, original voices and inventive theatrical sensibilities; plays that meld or leaven intelligent, serious statements with

quirky humor; plays that can engage and challenge at
the same time."

Application Specifics: Application form is available on Web site.
During the application period (most recently December-
February), fill out the form and mail with a one-page synopsis,
resume, and self-addressed, stamped envelope. Semifinalists
are then chosen and asked to send the full script.

Fees: A $15 fee for semifinalists.

Selection Criteria: "The subject matter is wide open, but I have
observed that 'historical' dramas, no matter how well-
written, tend not to fare as well in the vetting rounds as do
more unconventional, 'post-modern' plays. Instant turn-offs
include those plays I've already read a thousand times—like
the 'finding myself' plays—or really wordy, clunky plays,
frequently by converted novelists, that tend to tell everything
and show nothing. Also, plays whose politics are too obvious
or didactic, whose characters are distilled neatly into villains
and heroes, and—I think this is important—plays that are so
badly typed that I conclude the author doesn't give a damn
about his/her product. One more thing: If your play requires
six Asian children—or, say, a seven-foot-tall woman who can
sing basso profundo while juggling raccoons—we can't cast
it. That may be our fault, but we just can't do it."

Payments/Profits/Benefits: A $750 prize and paid travel expenses
so that the winning playwright can attend a week of final
rehearsals and opening night. Also, Trustus is incredibly helpful about helping plays get published. (Tuttle knows the
editors at Samuel French, the Dramatists Play Service, and
Playscripts, Inc., and will submit winning scripts himself with
lots of lavish endorsement.) Winning scripts have gone on to
productions at the Humana Festival and Off-Broadway.

Physical Production Details: The theater is essentially set up as
a big living room—seating consists of ninety-six Barcaloungers.
Patrons munch popcorn and there's a bar. Stage

dimensions: 25" × 30" with no curtain. Lighting: Seventy dimmers with a 2500-watt capacity apiece. Sound: a stage system with speaker.

Housing: One week's lodging at a local hotel for the winning playwright prior to opening night.

Past Artists/Productions of Note: *A Show of Hands* by David Lindsay-Abaire, *The Transparency of Val* by Stephen Belber, *Hook & Eye* by Andrea Lepico, *Kudzu* by Sarah Hammond, and *No Place Like Home* by Peter Morris.

Festival Flavor: "Certainly, the cast is eager to meet (and please) the playwright, and usually, between the newness of the product and the media stuff going on—newspaper and television interviews, cocktail parties, etc.—there's a lot of excitement in the air," says Tuttle.

The Bottom Line: A wonderful forum! The Trustus staff deeply respects playwrights and goes that extra mile to show off material to its best advantage.

Vital Theatre Company's Vital Signs

Founded: circa 2000

Contact Info: Vital Theatre Company, Literary Department, 432 West 42nd Street, New York, NY 10036. (212) 268-2040 (phone); (212) 268-0474 (fax)

E-mail: scripts@vitaltheatre.org; vital@vitaltheatre.org

Web site: *www.vitalsigns.org*

Performance Dates: Semiannually in November-December.

The Festival's Mission: To encourage emerging theater artists. Vital has presented the talents of almost 700 thespians. In addition to its regular season and the Vital Signs new works fest, Vital produces chamber opera and drag cabaret at the holidays.

Application Specifics: All genres considered. Submit full script (short plays only) with a brief synopsis, your bio/resume, a detailed production history of your project, and a cover letter with complete contact info. You may submit the name of a director you'd like to interpret the work as well (or, if your work's chosen, Vital will assign one of its directors to the piece). Check out the Web site above for submission info updates.

Fees: None.

Selection Criteria: To Vital's credit, the new works they select for the festival are extremely varied in terms of style and contact. Recent festival productions have tackled topics ranging from executions to racism.

Payment/Profits/Benefits: A full production in the festival.

Physical Production Details: A coveted Theatre Row perform-ance space. If chosen, inquire about tech specifics.

Housing: If chosen, inquire about availability.

Past Artists/Productions of Note: *Morphs* by Ty Adams; *The Honey Makers* by Deborah Grimberg; many, many others.

Festival Flavor: Very fun and eclectic in terms of a fascinating, wide range of artists to network and mingle with. The theater's prime location in midtown Manhattan means that the possibil-ity of a commercial producer checking out your work is very real—so get ready to solicit. Reviewers (such as the "Off-Off Broadway Review") do attend this fest, and participating playwrights have gotten some nice, lengthy write-ups.

The Bottom Line: A solid showcase for your work in NYC.

Women's Playwriting Festival

Founded: 1992

Contact Info: Rebecca Wolff, WPF Coordinator, Perishable Theatre, Perishable Theatre Arts Center, P.O. Box 23132, 95 Empire Street, Providence, RI 02903
(401) 331-2695 (phone); (401) 331-7811 (fax)
E-mail: wpf@perishable.org
Web site: *www.perishable.org*

Performance Dates: Annually; see Web site for current performance date info.

The Festival's Mission: Founded by Kathleen Jenkins, WPF is dedicated to provided a consistent forum for female writers to see their work performed.

Application Specifics: One-acts by female playwrights focusing on issues important in and to women's lives considered. See current guidelines at the following Web site: *www.aboutWPF.com*.

Fees: Contact the fest by e-mail at the above address for current guidelines.

Selection Criteria: Diverse stories from a diverse geographical range of authors are sought. The festival's quality quotient is extremely high, and it's competitive: Recent submissions for one festival tallied up at almost 300 from writers in eleven different countries. Three finalists are selected from those kinds of numbers for the festival.

Payments/Profits/Benefits: The winning author gets $500 in cash, and her script is given a fully staged one-month run during the festival. All finalists' scripts are published in an anthology, and each receives fifty copies of the publication (which also includes written script critiques by scholars associated with Perishable).

Physical Production Details: A seventy-five-seat black box fully equipped with light and sound, plus a 494.5-square-foot rehearsal space, and an additional 1253.75-square-foot dance studio space.

Housing: If chosen, inquire about availability.

Past Artists/Productions of Note: Carson Kreitzer, Bridget Carpenter, Alice Tuan, Jean Tay, and Carolyn Gage.

Festival Flavor: This fest is held in high esteem by the theater community as a whole, and female theater artists in particular. Famed playwright Theresa Rebeck has delivered the keynote address that kicks off the fest.

The Bottom Line: An ideal way to get your voice heard.

Section 4

Honorable Mentions

Here are a select group of more terrific festivals to present your work at. Please note that these only scratch the surface of quality forums that might be a perfect match for you. Seek out more by using an Internet search engine like Google.

Fringe Festivals

Athabasca Country Fringe Festival, 500-43 St., Athabasca, AB T9S 1M1 Canada
—A top Canada Fringe circuit pick.

Atlantic Fringe Festival, 11 Fourth Street, Dartmouth, NS B2X 1Y1 Canada (902) 435-4837 (phone)
—A top Canada fringe circuit pick.

Bath Fringe Festival, UK, Bath Fringe, 103 Walcot Street, BATH Somerset BA1 5BW England

admin@bathfringe.co.uk (e-mail), *www.bathfringe.co.uk* (Web site)
—This fringe is historic and respected. (Its roots wind back to
the festival world's "golden age" in the 1990s.)

Brighton Fringe Festival, UK, Brighton Fringe, Ground Floor, The
Argus Lofts, Kensington Street, Brighton BN1 4AJ England
01273 699733/699044 (phone), fringe@brighton.co.uk (e-mail),
www.brightonfringe.net (Web site)
—A supportive forum for grassroots artists in the UK.

Calgary Fringe Festival, 1229-9th Ave., S.E. Calgary, AB T2G 0S9
Canada (403) 265-3378, fringe@loosemoose.com (e-mail),
www.calgaryfringe.com (Web site)
—A top Canadian fringe circuit pick.

Cincinnati Fringe Festival, *www.cincyfringe.com*
—A promising new American festival.

Cowichan Fringe Festival, Box 764, Duncan, BC V9L 3Y1
Canada (250) 709-1440 (phone), fringe@cowichanfringe.com
(e-mail) *www.cowichanfringe.com* (Web site)
—A top Canadian fringe circuit pick.

The Grand Little Fringe, Box 21264, Grand Prairie, AB T8V
6W7 Canada
—A top Canadian fringe circuit pick.

Hong Kong Fringe Festival, 2 Lower Albert Rd., Central Hong
Kong, 852 2521 7251 (phone), *www.hkfringe.com*
—A colorful and exotic fringe; works with English-speaking artists.

Houston Fringe Festival, c/o Theater LaB Houston, P.O. Box
70755, Houston, TX 77270

(713) 868-5516 (phone), *www.theaterlabhouston.com* (Web site)
—A small but mighty stalwart with a loyal following.

London Fringe Festival, 474 Richmond Street, London ON N6A
3E6 Canada (519) 434-0606 (phone), londonfringe@bellnet.ca
(e-mail), *www.londonfringe.ca* (Web site)
—A top Canadian fringe circuit pick.

Melbourne Fringe Festival, Australia
info@melbournefringe.org.au (e-mail); *www.melbournefringe.org.au*
(Web site)
—An international tourist mecca with great local flavor.

Saskatoon International Fringe Festival, 600-245 3rd Avenue
South, Saskatoon, SK S7K 1M4 Canada
(306) 664-2239 (phone), *www.25thstreettheatre.com/fringe*
(Web site)
—A top Canadian fringe circuit pick.

Seoul Fringe, South Korea, Seoul Fringe Network Office,
2F #372-6, Seokyo Dong, Mapo-gu, Seoul, South Korea
121-83882-2-325-8150 (phone), 82-2-325-8992 (fax),
seoulfringe@hanmail.net (e-mail), *www.seoulfringe.net* (Web site)
—Very considerate and solicitous of American/European artists.

Thunder Bay Fringe Festival, 15-4A S. Court St., Thunder Bay,
ON P7B 2W4 Canada
(807) 344-1343 (phone), *www.tbfringe.com* (Web site)
—A top Canadian fringe circuit pick.

Performance-Driven Festivals

The Berlin Theater Festival (Berliner Festspiele), Germany, Berlin
Festival, P.O. Box 15 01 69, 10663 Berlin, Germany

+49 (0) 30-25489-0 (phone), *www.berlinerfestspiele.com* (Web site)
—This well-respected fest encourages artistic exchange between international playmakers at every career level.

Fierce! Fierce Earth Festival, UK, Fierce Earth, Unit 608b The Big Peg, 120 Vyse Street, Birmingham B18 6NF England
+44 (0) 121 244 8080 (phone), +44 (0) 121 244 8081 (fax), fierce@fierceearth.com (e-mail), *www.fierceearth.com* (Web site)
—Performance art at its best; Lydia Lunch put it on the map.

Festival of Alternate Theatrical Expression, Zagreb, Croatia
faki007@net.hr (e-mail) *www.attack.hr/faki* (Web site)
—Ultra-experimental gathering of theater renegades from countries worldwide.

Melbourne International Comedy Festival, Australia
info@comedyfestival.com.au (e-mail), *www.comedyfestival.com.au* (Web site)
—Lots of scouts come to watch great international comics strut their stuff here.

Playwrights' Festivals

Maine Playwrights' Festival, (207) 766-3386
   A small but worthwhile place to get your work noticed.

Nantucket Short Play Festival, Nantucket Theatrical Productions, Box 2177, Nantucket, MA 02584 (508)
228-5002 (phone)
—Known for spotlighting some of the best New England writing talent.

National Playwrights' Festival, c/o Florida Studio Theatre, 1241 North Palm Avenue, Sarasota, Florida 34236

(941) 366-9017 (phone), *www.fst2000.org* (Web site)
—An acclaimed festival for established writers.

Pittsburgh New Works Festival
(412) 881-6888 (phone), *www.pittsburghnewworks.org* (Web site)
—A nurturing, encouraging forum.

Rosetta Festival of New Works, Brass Tacks Theatre, 34-50 41st
Street #C2, Astoria, NY 11101
(212) 560-7261 (phone), info@brasstackstheatre.com (e-mail),
www.brasstackstheatre.com (Web site)
—A well-attended annual showcase in NYC.

Samuel French Off-Off Broadway Short Play Festival, Samuel
French Co., 45 West 25th Street, New York, NY 10010
(212) 206-8990 (phone)
—One of the best opportunities around to get published.

APPENDIX A

Cast of Characters

Melody Brooks, artistic director of the New Perspectives Theatre Company, is an esteemed director of Shakespearean works, as well as original scripts. She has worked at festivals and theaters worldwide with many respected artists, including Joseph Chaikin, Joanne Akalaitis, Anthony Zerbe, and Salome Jens, and teaches at Long Island University.

Shannan Calcutt, creator and performer of the Fringe favorite clown Izzy, recently made the short film "Chunk." Learn more about her work at *www.iamizzy.com*.

Leah Cooper, executive director of the Minnesota Fringe Festival, started her career at the fest as a passionate supporter of the Fringe. She then became a Fringe playwright, producer, and director, subsequently moving on to positions on the board of directors, then as board chair and interim managing director, before assuming her current post.

TJ Dawe, "King of the Fringe," is a highly respected touring writer/performer/director throughout North America. His credits include *Tired Clichés, Labrador,* and *One-Man Lord of the Rings Trilogy* (as director). Learn more about his work at *www.tjdawe.com.*

David Fuller is Artistic Director of the Jean Cocteau Repertory in New York City, as well as a noted actor, director, and critic.

Charles Fee, artistic director/producer of both of the Great Lakes Theatre Festival and the Idaho Shakespeare Festival, was trained as an actor at ACT and the University of San Diego. He is a noted stage director as well.

Christopher Lee Gibson, executive director of the Orlando Fringe Festival, describes himself as "a stage actor, producer, and director with little formal education and a wealth of personal experience, gained through a life in the arts." He started at the Orlando Fringe as a performer in 2000, then joined the staff as associate producer in 2001. That same year, he moved up to executive director.

Patrick Goddard, former general manager of the Montreal Fringe, is also a distinguished writer and performer of solo work. He was nominated for Best Actor at Edinburgh in 2002, and for his work at the Montreal Fringe, he received (with festival producer Jeremy Hechtman) a 2002 Montreal English Critics' Circle Award for Distinction.

Steven Gove is co-founder and director of the Prague Fringe Festival.

Matt Grabowski, founder of the Seattle Festival of Improv Theatre, is a highly respected improv scene performance veteran.

Paul Gudgin, director of the Edinburgh Festival Fringe, has extensive experience working in the field of music festivals as well.

Stella Hall, director of the Belfast Festival at Queen's University in Ireland, spent the majority of her working life in the arts working in Manchester, in the north of England, and also working across the UK—founding an arts center, running a venue, and working with agencies. She ran the largest arts center outside of London in the UK.

Sabrina Hamilton, artistic director of the Ko Fest of Performance, has worked in the United States and internationally as a distinguished lighting designer, production designer, performer, stage manager, and assistant director. Her credits include work with Mabou Mines, the New York Shakespeare Festival, the Goodman Theatre, the Mark Taper Forum, and festivals worldwide. She also served as route lightning designer for Greenwich Village's world-famous Halloween Parade for six years.

Kim Peter Kovac, senior program director for youth and family programs at the Kennedy Center in Washington, D.C., is co-head of New Visions, New Voices and an esteemed theater artist in her own right.

Fergus Linehan is director of the Dublin Theatre Festival.

Jenny Magnus, co-founder of the Curious Theatre Branch, the Rhinoceros Theater Festival, and the Curious School, has had work produced at the Museum of Contemporary Art, Steppenwolf, the Chicago Cultural Center, Theater on the Lake, and Gallery 37 Storefront in Chicago, among other venues. She was named one of the Chicago Tribune's 1998 Artists of the Year and one of New City Chicago's 50 Most Influential Artists (2001–3).

She received an artist's fellowship from the Illinois Arts Council in 1997, and is an adjunct professor at Columbia College.

Joseph V. Melillo, is the executive producer of the Brooklyn Academy of Music.

Thomas Morrissey, artistic director of the Genesius Guild, was a member of Circle Rep, and is a veteran freelance director.

Janet Munsil, producer of Intrepid Theatre, the Victoria Fringe, and the Uno Festival of Solo Performance, is a playwright whose work has been produced worldwide, including in the West End.

Trey Nichols, literary director for Moving Arts, is also an actor, director, and playwright who formerly served as Festival Director for the Edge of the World Theater Festival.

Nigel Redden, general director of the Spoleto Festival, also heads the Lincoln Center Festival.

Charlie Ross is a festival veteran who has written and performed numerous touring works, including the *One-Man Star Wars* and *One-Man Lord of the Rings* trilogies. Learn more about his work at *www.onemanstarwars.com*.

Zan Sawyer-Dailey, artistic manager at Actors Theatre of Louisville and one of the chief forces behind the Humana Festival of New American Plays, has a background in acting, teaching, and arts management. She's been associated with ATL since 1985.

Mark Scharf, chairman of the Baltimore Playwrights' Festival, is also an actor and award-winning playwright. His work has been presented at the Source Theatre and Signature Theatre Company in the Washington, D.C., area, and the William Renfield, the Inner Space, the Miranda Theatre Company, and the Polaris Theatre Company, among many others, in New York City. He has won the BPF fest multiple times himself, has worked with television producer Stephen J. Cannell, and has had his work produced worldwide.

Kirsten Schrader, acting executive artistic director of the Vancouver Fringe Festival, made her name in Canadian theater by directing and producing Eve Ensler's *The Vagina Monologues* at the Frederick Wood Theatre in conjunction with the international women's aid group V-Day. She has worked in the theater and film communities of Victoria, Vancouver, Toronto, Munich, and Freiburg, Germany.

Kate Snodgrass is co-founder and artistic director of the Boston Theatre Marathon at the Boston Playwrights' Theatre, Boston University.

Nick Stucchio, co-founder and artistic director of the Philadelphia Fringe Festival, was a dancer in the Pennsylvania Ballet from 1989–95. He is also the proud father of Carlo, Luca, and Ella.

Jason R. Teeter, artistic director of the Rainbow Theatre Festival, the festival's Lambda Project, and founder/artistic director of the Bread and Water Theatre, is also an actor, director, and frequently produced playwright.

Daniella Topol, director of the National Alliance for Musical Theatre's New Works program, holds an undergraduate degree in directing and a graduate degree in arts management from Carnegie-Mellon University. Her festival experience began at the

Lincoln Center Festival; she also served as associate producing director of the City Theatre in Pittsburgh.

Jon Tuttle, literary manager at the Trustus Theatre, won the Trustus Playwrights' Festival himself twice before becoming the company's Playwright-in-Residence.

Sue Zizza is executive director of the Nationals Audio Theatre Festivals. In addition, she is an instructor at New York University, and an independent, award-winning theater producer/sound designer.

APPENDIX B

Canadian Association of Fringe Festival Members

The following festivals are members of CAFF (North American Fringe Circuit), including some festivals located in the United States.

Orlando International Fringe Festival

Ottawa International Fringe Festival

Toronto Fringe Festival

Thunder Bay Fringe Festival

Minnesota Fringe Festival

Saskatoon International Fringe

Montreal Fringe Festival

Fraser Valley Fringe Festival

Winnipeg Fringe Festival

Athabasca Country Fringe Festival

The Grand Little Fringe

Lloydminster Fringe Festival

London Fringe Festival

Prince George Fringe

Festival Calgary Fringe Festival

San Francisco Fringe Festival

Cowichan Fringe Festival

Peterborough Fringe Festival

Edmonton Fringe Festival

Victoria Fringe Festival

Atlantic Fringe Festival

Vancouver Fringe Festival

APPENDIX C

Contact Information: Associations and Organizations

Here is a listing of some national theater arts assistance organizations you may wish to contact for resource information and advice.

Americans for the Arts (New York City)
1 East 53rd Street
New York, NY 10022
(212) 223-2787, (212) 753-1325
www.artsusa.org

Americans for the Arts (Washington, D.C.)
1000 Vermont Avenue NW 12th Floor
Washington, D.C. 20005
(202) 371-2830, (202) 371-0424 (fax)

American Theater Wing
250 West 57th Street, Suite 519
New York, NY 10107
(212) 869-5470

Association of Theatre for Children and Young People
724 Second Avenue South
Nashville, TN 37210
USASITE@aol.com
www.assitej-USA.org

Black Theatre Network c/o Kuntu Rep Theatre
3T01 Wesley W. Posvar Hall
230 S. Bouguet Street
Pittsburgh, PA 15260
rroebuck@pitt.edu

Institute of Outdoor Drama
CB#3240
University of North Carolina
Chapel Hill, NC 27599-3240
(919) 962-1328
(919) 962-4212 (fax)
outdoor@unc.edu
www.UNC.edu

The League of American Theatres and Producers
226 West 47th Street
New York, NY 10036
(212) 764-1122

National Endowment for the Arts
1100 Pennsylvania Avenue NW
Washington, D.C. 20506
(212) 682-5400

Performing Arts Resources
dbradypar@aol.com

Stage Managers Association
P.O. Box 22
Times Square Station
New York, NY 10108-2020
(212) 543-956734

Theatre Communications Group (TCG)
355 Lexington Avenue, 4th Floor
New York, NY 1007
(212) 697-5230
www.tcg.org

Theatre Development Fund
1501 Broadway, 21st Floor
New York, NY 10036
(212) 221-0885

The Theatre Guild
226 West 47th Street
New York, NY 10036
(212) 221-0885

University/Resident Theatre Association
1560 Broadway, Suite 141
New York, NY 10036
(212) 221-1130, (212) 869-2752 (fax)
URTA2aol.com
www.URTA.com

United States Institute for Theatre Technology
6443 Ridings Road
Syracuse, NY 13206-111
(315) 463-6463, (315) 463-6525 (fax)
www.USITT.org

Volunteer Lawyers for the Arts
1 East 53rd Street, 6th Floor
New York, NY 10022
(212) 319-2787 (information directory), (212) 319-2910 (legal matters line), (212) 752-6575 (fax)
vlany@bway.net
www.vlany.org

APPENDIX D

Contact Information: Unions

Actors Equity Association (National Headquarters)
165 West 46th Street
New York, NY 10036
(212) 869-8530

Actors Equity Association (Los Angeles)
5757 Wilshire Blvd., Suite 1
Los Angeles, CA 90036
(323) 634-1750

Actors Equity Association (Chicago)
203 North Wabash Avenue, Suite 1700
Chicago, IL 60601
(312) 641-0393

Actors Equity Association (San Francisco)
235 Pine Street, Suite 1200
San Francisco, CA 94104
(415) 391-3830

Actors Equity Association (Orlando, Florida)
10369 Orangewood Boulevard
Orlando, Florida 32821
(407) 345-8600

American Guild of Variety Artists
184 Fifth Avenue, 6th Floor
New York, NY 10010
(212) 675-1003

Association of Authors' Representatives
10 Astor Place, 3rd Floor
New York, NY
(212) 353-3709

The Dramatists Guild, Inc.
234 West 44th Street
New York, NY 10036
(212) 398-9366

Educational Theatre Association
2343 Auburn Avenue
Cincinnati, OH 45219-2819
(513) 421-3900
www.edta.org

Society of Stage Directors and Choreographers
1501 Broadway, 17th Floor
New York, NY 10036
(212) 391-1070

APPENDIX E

Publications

Consult the following publications for consistently helpful information about the business of theater. Subscription contact info is listed below; also check newsstands for a number of these titles.

The Agencies Guides
P.O. Box 3899
Hollywood, CA 90078

American Theatre Magazine c/o Theatre Communications Group
355 Lexington Avenue
New York, NY 10017
(212) 697-5230
www.tcg.com

Back Stage/Back Stage West/Drama-Logue
1 (800) 437-3183

Black Talent News
1620 Centinela Avenue, Suite 204
Englewood, CA 90302
www.blacktalentnews.com

Call Board
870 Market Street, Suite 375
San Francisco, CA 94102
(415) 430-1140

Dramatics Magazine
Educational Theatre Association
2343 Auburn Avenue
Cincinnati, Ohio 45219-2815
www.edta.org

Hollywood Reporter
5055 Wilshire Boulevard
Los Angeles, CA 90036
(213) 525-2000

Performing Arts Magazine
Performing Arts Network
10350 Santa Monica Blvd.
Los Angeles, CA 90025

Southern Theatre Magazine
Southeastern Theatre Conference
P.O. Box 9868
Greensboro, NC 27429-0868
www.setc.org/pubs.html

Stage Directions Magazine
110 William Street, 23rd Floor
New York, NY 10031

Theatrical Index
888 Eighth Avenue
New York, NY 10019
(212) 585-6343

Variety/Daily Variety
5700 Wilshire Boulevard, Suite 120
Los Angeles, CA 90036-5804
(323) 965-4476

Index

Books from Allworth Press

Allworth Press is an imprint of Allworth Communications, Inc. Selected titles are listed below.

Building the Successful Theater Company
by Lisa Mulcahy (paperback, 6 × 9, 240 pages, $19.95)

Making It on Broadway: Actor's Tales of Climbing to the Top
by David Wiener and Jodie Langel (paperback, 6 × 9, 288 pages, $19.95)

The Stage Producer's Business and Legal Guide
by Charles Grippo (paperback, 6 × 9, 256 pages, $19.95)

Technical Theater for Nontechnical People, Second Edition
by Drew Campbell (paperback, 6 × 9, 288 pages, $19.95)

Business and Legal Forms for Theater
by Charles Grippo (paperback, 8 1/2 × 11, 192 pages, $29.95)

Career Solutions for Creative People: How to Balance Artistic Goals with Career Security
by Dr. Ronda Ormont (paperback, 6 × 9, 320 pages, $19.95)

Acting That Matters
by Barry Pineo (paperback, 6 × 9, 256 pages, $19.95)

Improv for Actors
by Dan Diggles (paperback, 6 × 9, 224 pages, $19.95)

Mastering Shakespeare: An Acting Class in Seven Scenes
by Scott Kaiser (paperback, 6 × 9, 256 pages, $19.95)

Movement for Actors
edited by Nicole Potter (paperback, 6 × 9, 288 pages, $19.95)

Promoting Your Acting Career: A Step-by-Step Guide to Opening the Right Doors, Second Edition
by Glenn Alterman (paperback, 6 × 9, 240 pages, $19.95)

An Actor's Guide—Making It in New York City
by Glenn Alterman (paperback, 6 × 9, 288 pages, $19.95)

Running Theaters: Best Practices for Leaders and Managers
by Duncan M. Webb (paperback, 6 × 9, 256 pages, $19.95)